HOMEMADE HEALTHY DOG FOOD COOKBOOK

365-Days of Quick & Affordable Recipes to Keep Your Puppy Healthy and Fit (20 Delicious Treats Included)

TABLE OF CONTENTS

INTRODUCTION 9

CHAPTER 1: What You Need To Know To Make Your Own Dog Food 10

CHAPTER 2: Homemade Dog Food Recipes 16

   Beef-Based Recipes 17

      Beef Meat Balls 17

      Beef & Fish Rice 17

      Beef Stew 18

      Green Eggs & Beef 19

      Turmeric Beef 19

   Chicken Based Recipes 20

      Chicken Broccoli & Rice 20

      Fruity Chicken 21

      Oats & Chicken 21

      Crock-Pot Sweet Potato & Chicken 22

      Sage Chicken & Sweet Potato 22

   Fish-Based Recipes 24

      Fish Fry 24

      Tahini Fish 25

      Oregano & Parsley Fish 26

      Salmon Medley 26

      Tuna Balls 27

      Chicken, Apple, Leafy Medley 28

      Kale Nachos 28

      Triple Three 29

      Chicken Hummus 29

      Beef Squares 30

      Ginger & Pumpkin Smash 30

      Yogurt Blend 31

      Chicken & Yogurt 31

      Turkey Turmeric 31

      Tummy Medley 32

Pumpkin Based Recipes 33

- Pumpkin Mix 33
- Pumpkin & Squash 34
- Pumpkin Balls 34
- Pumpkin & Berry Oatmeal 35
- Pumpkin Seeds & Turkey 35
- Peanut Butter & Chicken 36
- Sweet Potato & Peanut Butter 36
- Peanut Butter Oatmeal 37
- Peanut Butter Banana Balls 37
- Peanut Butter Mix 38

Homemade Dog Food Recipes for Dogs with Arthritis, Hip & Joint Ailments 39

- Rosehip and Nettle Beef Stew 39
- Pumpkin Turmeric Treats 40
- Chicken Beef Patties 40
- Venison Meal 41
- Orange Chicken 41
- Tuna and Shrimp 42

Homemade Dog Food for Dogs with Diabetes 43

- Chicken and Vegetable Meal 43
- Chicken Stew 44
- Chuck and Barley Stew 44
- Beef and Cottage Cheese Meal 45

Homemade Food for Dogs with Digestive Disorders 46

- Chicken Casserole 46
- Sweet Potato and Beef Stew 47
- Minced Chicken and Rice 47
- Chicken Neck Soup 48
- Beef, Barley, and Broccoli 49
- Chicken and Rice 49
- Tapioca and Tofu 50
- Beef in the Slow Cooker 50
- Chicken, Eggs, and Rice 51

Homemade Dog Food Recipes for Dogs having Kidney disease 51

- Beef and Tofu 51

Homemade Dog Food Recipes for Dogs having live disorders 52
Beef and Brown Rice Dinner 52
White Rice and Beef 52

Homemade Dog Food for Improving Skin and Coat Health 53
Peanut Butter and Fish Oil Treats 53

Homemade Dog Food for Increasing Weight 54
Chicken, Beef, and Oats 54

Homemade Low-fat" Dog Food Recipes 55
Homemade Beef Dinner 55
Homemade Chicken Dinner 55
Ground Beef Recipe 56
Doggie low-fat dessert 56
Homemade Fish Dinner 56
Doggie Chili 57
Mixed Meat Goodness 57
Cheesy Beef with Rice 58
Chicken with Broccoli and Rice 58
Raw Chicken Dinner 59

Homemade Hypoallergenic Dog Food Recipes 60
Basic Chicken plus Rice recipe 60
Sweet Chicken 60
Chicken and Potato Recipe 61
Turkey With Veggies 61
Eggs and Cheese Mild Homemade Recipe 62
Fish-Veggie Patty 62
Homemade Kibble Recipe 62
Ground Round Dog Food 63
Cheese and Chicken Dinner 63
Doggie Peanut Butter Delight 64

Dog Food Recipes for Senior Dogs 65
Doggie's Stew 65
Scaled-down Doggie's Stew 66
Chili Goodness 66
Chicken Soup Cookies 66

    Beef Delight 67

    Veggies and Chicken 67

    Frosty Paws 67

    Oldie but Goldie 68

    Raw Fish Delight 68

Homemade Breakfast for Dogs 69

    Egg Breakfast of Champions 69

Home-Made Dinner for Dogs 69

    Chicken, Broccoli & Rice Dinner 69

    Beef Balls Dinner for Dogs 70

Homemade Raw Food for Dogs 70

    Grain-Free Raw Dog Food 70

Meaty Homemade Dog Food 71

    Slow-Cooked Canine Chicken 71

    Raw Chicken Dinner 71

    Salmon Balls 72

    Sardine Cakes 72

    Beef Fried Rice 73

    Terrier's Tuna Casserole 74

    Chicken and Rice Tender Tummy Meal 74

    Stuffed Pumpkin 75

    Salmon and Spinach Hash 75

    Lamb Hash 76

    Buffalo Meatballs 76

    Turkey Kibble 77

    Chicken and Sardine Kibble 78

    Buffalo Hash 79

    Chicken Meatloaf 79

    Mutt Meatloaf Meal 80

    Raw Meatloaf 81

Raw Power Homemade Dog Food Recipes 81

    Spot's Spinach and Sprats 81

    Mini Liver Quiche 82

    Baked Egg Cup 82

    Chia Seed Oatmeal 83

Spinach Omelet 84

Cottage Cheese Breakfast 84

Fishermen's Eggs 85

Raw Breakfast 85

Deviled Eggs 86

Homemade Dog Side Dishes 87

Pepitas 87

Kanine Kale and Kiwi 88

Arroz con Pollo 88

Chicken for Pulping's 89

Cluck and Quinoa Casserole 89

Poultry Palooza 90

Chicken Thighs and Tabbouleh 90

Slow-Cooked Chicken and Barley 91

Stir-Fry and Rice 91

Turkey Minestrone 92

Lazysagne 92

Turkey Meat Loaf 93

Beef and Bulgur 94

Hearty Beef 94

Dog Treat Recipes 95

Peanut Butter Cookies 95

Cheddar Dog Biscuits 96

Dog snacks made with peanut butter and pumpkin 96

Pumpkin Ginger Dog Biscuit 97

Chunk Chicken and Sweet Potato Treats 98

Microwave Oatmeal Balls 98

Peanut Butter, Honey, and Oat Cookies 99

Sunflower Sensations 99

Quick-and-Easy Cheese Circles 100

Birthday Blueberry Pup cakes 101

Valentine Hearts 102

Potato Cranberry Christmas Cookies 102

Striped Peppermint Christmas Canes 103

Peppermint Christmas Cookies 104

Chicken Liver Treats 105

Bisquick and Beef Treats 105

Basic Bones 106
  Beefy Bacon Dog Bones 107
  Crispy Cheese Circles 107
  Flaxseed Twists 108

CONCLUSION 110

INTRODUCTION

When it comes to dog food, there is a huge debate about whether or not to prepare your own, to give your dog raw food, to use only natural products, and whether or not to follow the AAFCO (the Association of American Feed Control Officials) criteria for good nutrition.

Because no two people or dogs are the same, no one diet or method of food preparation is appropriate for all. Let us help you figure out what's best for you! Doing this will expand your mind and prompt you to ask more questions.

In this book, we will go through some of the benefits of making your own dog food! Then we'll provide you with 150 recipes for making your own dog chow as well as 20 recipes for making treats for your furry friend.

Buying and preparing your own food will almost certainly result in higher-quality meals. You'll always know exactly where your meat comes from and how fresh it is when you do this. Consider using organic and grass-fed beef in your homemade dog food recipes, but don't feel terrible if you can't afford it; the most crucial thing is to be concerned about what your dog is eating.

In the case of dogs with digestive issues, there are many reasons to experiment with new foods or new methods of preparation for them. Switching to a more natural diet may be the solution.

Preparing your own dog food guarantees that your dog isn't getting artificial components and vitamins, like vitamin K3, which is the synthetic counterpart of vitamin K1. Vitamin K3 can cause a major health danger if taken in excess. In addition, you don't want your dog consuming meat by-products, either.

CHAPTER 1:
What You Need To Know To Make Your Own Dog Food

Ingredients for Homemade Dog Foods

What Ingredients should you use to create your dog's food from scratch?

Quality Dog Food Proteins

Dogs should consume at least half of their diets consisting of meat, particularly white meat unless they are active! Dogs are often given bones. However, some people advise against giving them cooked bones.

Salmon

Adding salmon to your dog's food may be done in various ways, from adding it to a pre-made, all-natural, store-bought dish to making your own. Salmon is high in zinc and other essential elements, making it an excellent addition to your dog's diet. Vitamin D, which is found in fish, is an important nutrient. You'll need to supplement the vitamin if you don't give your dog fish.

Liver

It is suggested that tiny quantities of the liver be fed daily. The liver of beef or chicken is an excellent addition to any homemade dog food recipe. Add an ounce of the liver for each pound of other animal Ingredients as a general rule of thumb when preparing dishes.

Eggs & Dairy

Eggs are an excellent source of protein, including other nutrients. Canines under 20 pounds should limit their egg consumption to one egg per day; larger dogs should limit their egg consumption to one egg every meal. Blend in the eggshells, too, if you'd want to add some texture. eggshells are rich sources of calcium, magnesium, phosphorus, and potassium

Even your dog may benefit from dairy products such as plain yogurt, kefir, cottage cheese, and ricotta cheese! Most individuals choose cottage and ricotta cheese because other varieties include too much fat.

Starches, Vegetables, & Fruits

Foods that are high in vegetables and starches are among the best for dogs. You may include a variety of fruits and vegetables in your dog food recipe. Adding a small number of starchy vegetables to a dog's diet may help preserve some flesh on their bones, but it's best to do so in moderate amounts. Cooking starchy foods is the best way to make them digestible for your dog.

Squash, pumpkin, and beans are all excellent alternatives to the more traditional root vegetables.

There are no calories in leafy greens. Thus, they can be fed in any amount! As a cautionary remark, excessive use might lead to gas. When feeding significant amounts of broccoli and cauliflower, it is best to boil them since they may interfere with thyroid function.

Bananas, apples, berries, melon, and papaya are all acceptable and healthful options for dogs, but grapes and raisins should be avoided since they may lead to renal failure.

A Word of Caution Regarding Grain

Grains are a hot-button issue. Some dogs can manage them, while others are not. Seizures and allergic rhinitis are just a few of the health issues they might cause because of their ability to exacerbate already existing inflammation. Remember to pay attention while adding these Ingredients when preparing your dog food. Whether starchy vegetables have the same effect is unknown.

If the thought of giving your dog grains makes you anxious, you may simply exclude the rice from your homemade dog food recipes.

A dog's diet should not include more than 50% of its calories from grains and starchy vegetables.

Supplements

A homemade dog chow recipe wouldn't be complete without the right supplements. Vitamin D, vitamin E, Iodine, and green mixes are just some nutrients your dog should be getting from his or her food.

When feeding your dog, a diet rich in these vitamins, it's difficult to know precisely how much and keep track of the amount. In many ways, it's identical to nursing a baby. Your kid (human or otherwise) should acquire the necessary vitamins and minerals, but they don't have to consume every single one of those nutrients. Dogs are in the same boat.

Although the AAFCO has set nutritional standards for dog food, they are thought to be the minimum your dog needs to live. Your objective in feeding your dog a customized diet is to strike a balance between providing enough nutrients to keep your dog alive and overfeeding and overdosing them.

Homemade Food Vs. Store Food

Most pet owners want to ensure that their dog has a long and happy life, and shifting to a homemade diet is an attempt to achieve that objective.

It was recently discovered in research conducted by the University of Guelph Ontario Veterinary College (UGOVC) in Canada that 87% of dog owners feed their canines human-grade food. Still, it's impossible to dismiss the importance of commercial dog food, which has been routinely supplied since the mid-1800s by an industry.

Do you think homemade or store-bought dog food is better for your pup? Here's a short side-by-side comparison to aid your decision-making process.

Fresh Ingredients

Homemade dog food is unquestionably the best. In order to give your dog, the freshest possible foods, you must make his meals yourself at home. The shelf life of most factory-made dog food is lengthy. Unsealed dry dog food may last up to 18 months; unsealed canned food can last up to two years. Every time you buy a new bag or can of food, you should check the expiration date.

Fresh dog food delivery companies like The Farmer's Dog, which promises meals delivered within days after preparation, nonetheless have some lag time. It is best to begin preparing your own dog food if you want to offer your pet the freshest Ingredients possible.

Nutritional value

While you would assume that homemade dog food is superior to commercially produced kibble, this isn't necessarily true. Because dogs' dietary requirements and digestion vary from those of humans, homemade meals may be deficient in the beneficial components that dogs need. At the University of California–Davis Veterinary Medicine, a study examined 200 common dog food recipes and found 95 percent of them to be lacking in at least one vital vitamin.

In contrast, every dog food produced in the United States must fulfil USDA guidelines for balanced nutrition. The Center for Veterinary Medicine is the US Food and Drug Administration division that oversees Ingredients. The implementation of state regulations governing the safe manufacturing and packaging of animal food is the responsibility of the Association of American Feed Control Officials.

Safety

As a result of a number of recalls in the previous 15 years, homemade dog food has become a growing trend. Around 180 pet food manufacturers voluntarily pulled their goods off the market in 2007 after reports surfaced that their products had caused renal damage or death in thousands of dogs and cats in the US and Canada.

Commercial dog food isn't the only source of foodborne disease. Only 2% of recorded foodborne disease incidents in 2010 were linked to pet food, according to 2010 research. That's compared to the 76 million instances of foodborne disease globally each year, which result in approximately 5,000 deaths.

You should also be aware of typical foods that might be unhealthy or even deadly to dogs while preparing meals for them. Avocado, chocolate, grapes, and raisins are all on the shortlist.

Cost

Are home-cooked meals for your dog less costly than buying them? The answer is that it is probably not. below are some things to remember:

Budget. From $1/lb. for dry kibble to over $20 for a 13-oz. container of dog food, costs may vary widely in the retail market. Calculate your current meal costs to get a clear idea of how much it will cost to make a move.

Ingredients. What will you need to make your own food if you decide to do so? Do you know how much they cost and whether they're accessible in your neighborhood? Although duck is often used in homemade dishes since it's cheaper than chicken and easier to get year-round, it's not always available.

Effort and time. What is the value of your time? Buying dog food at the store is a no-brainer: Open the bag and take out the appropriate quantity to serve. In comparison, making your dog food requires more time and work. Cooking and storing meals effectively take more than just purchasing the necessary components.

When deciding whether to give your dog store-bought or handmade food, there are many things to consider. Taking into account his age, health, and lifestyle, as well as your money and availability, is essential.

Carry out your research and discuss it with your veterinarian before making any decisions. Because of her extensive knowledge of canine health, she can help make informed choices about how to best care for your pet. Working together, you can feel confident that your dog is getting the greatest diet possible for his health, happiness, and long-term well-being.

What Food to Avoid for Your Dog

First and foremost, you need to be aware that certain items people consume should not be provided to your dog.

These are some things that you should not give your dog, among others:

- Alcohol
- Apple seeds
- Apricot pits
- Avocados
- Cherry pits
- Chocolate
- Coffee (and other caffeinated drinks)
- Garlic: Some people feed it in little quantities, although this should be done sparingly. Ask your veterinarian for suggestions.
- Grapes and raisins: Raisins are more harmful than grapes because of their condensed form; steer clear of cereals and pastries that include raisins.
- Macadamia nuts
- Nutmeg
- Onions

- Peach pits
- Persimmon seeds
- Plum pits
- Potato peels (green parts and eyes only; the rest of the skin is okay): Any potato parts that are green or sprouted should be discarded. All varieties of potatoes are included in this.
- Tea
- Yeast dough: Uncooked dough can be very dangerous to your dog.

Xylitol is a sweetener that is extremely toxic to dogs and is used in some diet foods and sugar-free gums.

Nutritional Considerations

For some pet owners, it can be challenging to maintain a balanced diet that will enable their animals to live their best lives. You might decide to prepare your dog's main diet from scratch after giving some of these recipes a try on your dog. The first step is to make an appointment with a veterinarian for your dog. Ask your veterinarian for advice on the transition and the best diets and supplements for your dog's size, age, activity level, and any health issues.

Remember, if you haven't discussed changing your dog's food with your veterinarian, be sure to do so. Without being aware of your dog's particular requirements, feeding homemade dog food might be a formula for disaster.

Vitamins & Minerals

While we can all agree that homemade dog food can be a fantastic source of vitamins and minerals. A good thing might be too much of a negative thing in this situation. When your dog consumes more of a certain dietary vitamin than his body needs, vitamin toxicity may result.

If it lasts for a long time, this may be a very significant issue that might even be fatal. If you attempt to serve your pet a nutritious dinner, you can unknowingly be doing more damage than good. For instance, vitamin A toxicity in dogs may cause fatal or irreversible bone damage.

This is why it's crucial that you collaborate with a qualified expert to develop a nutritional plan tailored to your dog's particular dietary requirements. You may modify these recipes, as well as any others you may uncover, to suit your pet's particular demands once you are aware of the rule that you must follow.

Consider the dietary information shown on the cereal box's back that you consumed for breakfast. We can observe how each meal we consume measures up to the nutritional guidelines for people by checking the nutritional information on the container. As we all know, there are specific dietary standards for humans.

Feed The Dog According to its Age

The development of an appropriate diet for your dog depends significantly on its stage of life. Puppies require more fat, protein, and calories in their food than adult dogs do. The nutritional requirements of dogs depend on their size; giant breed puppies require less calcium than their smaller counterparts.

When we feed pets, it's not that easy. The incredible diversity of the canine species is one of its outstanding features. The list includes large dogs, little dogs, athletic breeds, and slobbery puppies. It's hard to establish guidelines for the nutrients a dog needs to consume daily.

Consultation with your dog's veterinarian is the only way to be certain. Compared to pups, a senior dog may only need to consume 25% protein in his diet.

Working with a canine nutritionist can assist you in developing a strategy. It is their job to inform you how much protein, fruit, veg, carbs, and fat to put in your dog's meal. You can easily adjust recipes to match your dog's specific requirements once you know the ratio.

Find The Happy Medium

Did you know that the majority of nutritional components can be hazardous in either too much or too little quantity? Yes, health issues can result from taking a beneficial substance in excess. Here are some ideas to consider:

As they struggle to eliminate the extra protein the body cannot digest, your dog's kidneys and liver may become overworked from eating too much protein. (Puppy growth issues can result from inadequate protein intake)

Excess weight on your dog might result from eating too much fat in their diet! However, a lack of fat causes a dull coat and flaky skin.

Vitamin deficiencies will make your tail-wagging friend weak and exhausted, while vitamin overdoses can stress your dog's organs and even cause bladder stones.

Another crucial component of a balanced diet is fiber. Fiber overuse might result in gas. One food group in your pet's diet that is simple to detect (and suffer from) an imbalance is fiber.

As you can see, striking the appropriate balance entails a variety of criteria, yet doing so has significant advantages. You have complete control over the components that go into your dog's diet, and you may alter it to suit your dog's preferences.

CHAPTER 2:
Homemade Dog Food Recipes

Beef-Based Recipes

Beef Meat Balls

Ingredients

- 10 lb. of ground beef
- 10 eggs
- 1 ½ C. rice
- 3 C. of carrots and broccoli, chopped optional bread crumbs, and chopped parsley

Directions

1. Cook the rice and vegetables until soft.
2. Get a bowl large enough to combine all of the Ingredients in it. Stir well.
3. Scoop mixture into balls and arrange on a prepared baking sheet
4. A 40-minute baking period is required at a temperature of 400 degrees Fahrenheit.
5. Allow cooling before serving!

Beef & Fish Rice

Ingredients

- 4 lb. of ground beef
- 1 sweet potato
- 1 ⅓ C. white rice
- 1 can of mackerel
- 4 C. peas & carrots
- 6 eggs
- 6 egg shells
- 1 Tbsp. rosemary, chopped finely
- 1 Tbsp. ginger, finely chopped

Directions

1. Cook rice until it's tender
2. Fully cook the ground beef and drain all the fat
3. Use a fork to prick the sweet potato. microwave for 3 minutes
4. On a baking sheet, bake egg shells for 7 minutes at 350 degrees. Once baked, mix or crush the shells into a powder.
5. Add rosemary and ginger to mashed vegetables after steaming.
6. Remove the mackerel from the water.
7. Add the rest of the Ingredients with the eggs to the rice pot, and cook until the eggs are done.

Beef Stew

Ingredients:

- 1 ½ lb. of beef- any kind
- 1 sweet potato
- ½ C. of carrots

- ½ C. frozen peas
- 2 Tbsp. coconut oil
- Water

Directions:

1. Pan-fry the beef until well done, and drain off the oil from the pan
2. Use a fork to prick the sweet potato and microwave for 2 minutes at 50% power.
3. Cook the peas and carrots until they are tender.
4. Simmer for approximately 20 minutes, occasionally stirring, with just enough water to just cover the Ingredients.
5. Allow to cool before serving!

Green Eggs & Beef

Ingredients

- 2 lb. beef
- 5 eggs
- ¼ C. kelp powder
- 1 bunch of kale
- 1 C. broth

Directions

1. Thoroughly cook meat and remove any oil from the pan
2. Add kale and kelp to the broth and bring it to a boil, then lower the heat and simmer for 5 minutes.
3. Add the eggs and meat to the stock and simmer until the eggs are cooked through.
4. Serve and enjoy!

Turmeric Beef

Ingredients

- 2 lb. beef
- 1 lb. broccoli
- 1 C. white rice
- ¼ C. turmeric powder
- 2 Tbsp. coconut oil

Directions

1. Completely cook the meat
2. Prepare the rice by following the package Directions until it's tender.
3. Prepare broccoli by steaming it.
4. Add the rice and all of the other Ingredients.

Chicken Based Recipes

Chicken Broccoli & Rice

Ingredients

- 5 lb. chicken breasts
- 4 lb. broccoli, chopped
- 1 ¼ C. rice
- 2 Tbsp. olive oil

Directions

1. Completely cook the chicken breasts in boiling water.
2. While the chicken is cooking, cook the rice until it's tender.
3. Use a microwavable steamer to soften the broccoli.
4. Discard any remaining water and combine all of the Ingredients.

Fruity Chicken

Ingredients

- 2 lb. of chicken breasts
- 1 C. white rice
- ½ C. blueberries
- ½ C. pears
- ½ C. pitted cherries
- Optional cooked egg shells for extra calcium and nutrients

Directions

1. Cook the chicken until it's done.
2. Cook the rice until it is tender.
3. Cut fruit into small pieces.
4. Drain the water from the chicken and rice, then allow them to cool before combining them.

Oats & Chicken

Ingredients

- 2 lb. of chicken breast
- 1 C. rice
- ⅔ C. quick-cooking oats
- 2 C. spinach
- ½ C. carrots
- ½ C. plain yogurt
- ½ C. chopped parsley
- 2 Tbsp. olive oil

Directions

1. Cook the rice for 15 minutes or until it is tender.
2. When the chicken is done cooking, remove it from the water and set it aside.
3. When the vegetables are tender, steam them together and chop them finely.
4. Combine all of the Ingredients in a large mixing bowl.

Crock-Pot Sweet Potato & Chicken

Ingredients

- 2 lb. of chicken breast
- 1 sweet potato cut into chunks
- 1 C. rice
- ½ C. chopped green beans
- ½ C. chopped carrots
- 2 Tbsp. olive oil
- Optional 1 Tbsp. rosemary

Directions

1. For best results, cook chicken for 5 hours on high in a crockpot using all of the Ingredients listed above until all of the Ingredients are pliable.

Sage Chicken & Sweet Potato

Ingredients

- 2 lb. chicken
- 2 sweet potatoes

- ½ lb. of spinach
- About 15 sage leaves (or half a package)
- 4 Tbsp. olive oil

Directions

1. Cook the chicken until it's done.
2. Microwave sweet potato for 10 minutes after pricking it with a fork.
3. Add the sage leaves to a skillet of olive oil and sauté for 2 minutes on medium heat.
4. Continue to boil for a few more minutes until the spinach has wilted.
5. Slice and combine all of the items into a single dish.

Fish-Based Recipes

Fish Fry

Ingredients

- 2 lb. white fish (Cod or Swai)
- 2 cans pink salmon
- 2 eggs
- 1 C. zucchini
- ½ C. green beans
- ½ C. peas

Directions

1. Prepare fish according to the package Directions.
2. Boil the peas, green beans, and zucchini until they are tender.
3. Add the canned salmon and eggs to the vegetables
4. Finally, drain the water.
6. Combine all of the Ingredients and serve

Tahini Fish

Ingredients

- lb. white fish
- 1 C. broth
- 1 can of garbanzo beans
- 4 eggs
- 1 C. chopped carrots
- ½ C. tahini

Directions

1. Bake the fish until it is done completely
2. Simmer broth, carrots, and drained beans in a saucepan until carrots are tender
3. Add tahini and whisk
4. Toss in the eggs and let them cook.
5. Add everything and combine.

Oregano & Parsley Fish

Ingredients

- lb. white fish
- Sweet potato
- ½ lb. of green beans
- 4 Tbsp. oregano
- 4 Tbsp. parsley
- Tbsp. olive oil

Directions

1. Follow the package instructions for baking the fish.
2. Pierced the sweet potatoes using a fork and boiled in the microwave for 10 minutes or until they were tender.
3. Cook the green beans in a pot of boiling water until they are tender.
4. Serve it with the rest of the Ingredients!

Salmon Medley

Ingredients

- 2 lb. salmon
- 1 C. rice

- 1 C. peas
- ½ C. cauliflower

Directions

1. Bake the salmon (unless you are using canned).
2. Cook the rice until it is tender.
3. Vegetables should be steamed rather than boiled.
4. Combine the Ingredients in a large bowl.

Tuna Balls

Ingredients

- 2 lb. of canned tuna
- 1 C. rice
- eggs
- ½ lb. spinach
- Optional coconut oil and breadcrumbs

Directions

1. Cook the rice until it is tender.
2. Cook the eggs and spinach in the rice, occasionally stirring until the eggs are set and the spinach has wilted.
3. Mix everything together.
4. If the mixture is too dry, add a couple of teaspoons of coconut oil. If your pup's stomach can tolerate it, add a couple of tablespoons of breadcrumbs.
5. Form into balls and chill, or retain as a mixture and store in the refrigerator.

Chicken, Apple, Leafy Medley

Ingredients

- lb. chicken breast
- Eggs
- C. spinach
- 2 skinned apples
- 2 Tbsp. olive oil

Directions

1. In a stock pot, simmer the chicken until it's done.
2. Simmer for 10 minutes with everything else except the eggs.
3. Extinguish the flame and add the eggs.
4. Serve and preserve any leftovers once you've stirred everything together, and let it cool.

Kale Nachos

Ingredients

- 2 bunches of Kale
- 1 lb. ground beef
- Can black beans (no salt added)
- Tbsp. olive oil

Directions

1. Cook the meat until it is fully done, then drain the oil.
2. Mix ground beef with black beans.
3. Add 1–2 tsp. of olive oil to a different pan that is already hot over medium heat.

4. Place the kale leaves in a pan and remove the stems.
5. Toss kale in the skillet and cook it for approximately 10 minutes or until it's wilted and charred.
6. Mix ground beef and beans with greens, then serve.

Triple Three

Ingredients

- 1 lb. chicken
- 1 lb. beef
- 1 lb. canned salmon
- ½ lb. broccoli
- ½ lb. carrots
- ½ lb. peas
- Optional eggshells

Directions

1. Cook the meats until they're done.
2. Cook broccoli, carrots, and peas in a steamer.
3. Put everything together and serve!

Chicken Hummus

Ingredients

- 2 lb. chicken
- cans garbanzo beans
- ¼ C. tahini
- ¼ C. chopped carrots

- ¼ C. olive oil
- 2 Tbsp. kelp powder or any other type of green vitamin and chopped spinach can be added

Directions

1. Cook the chicken in a pot of boiling water until it is done.
2. Carrots should be steamed and chopped after they have finished cooking.
3. Wash the garbanzo beans well with water
4. Blend garbanzo beans, olive oil, tahini, kelp powder, and all of the other Ingredients until smooth
5. Blend or crush the Ingredients until they're smooth.
6. Mix the hummus with sliced carrots and chicken.
7. Serve!

Beef Squares

Ingredients

- lb. diced beef
- 3 C. any broth 2 eggs
- 1 lb. broccoli
- ½ lb. spinach

Directions

1. Cook the meat until it is fully done.
2. Steam some broccoli
3. Add chopped spinach and eggs to the boiling stock in a saucepan.
4. Serve it with the rest of the Ingredients!

Ginger & Pumpkin Smash

Ingredients

- 1 can all-natural pumpkin puree
- Approximately 1 Tbsp. of ginger (the number of spoons is based on the size of your dog)

Directions

1. Prepare the pumpkin, stirring in the ginger powder, until well combined.
2. Serve in little quantities.

Yogurt Blend

Ingredients

- 1 C. plain yogurt
- Pinch of ginger powder
- ½ C. pumpkin

Directions

1. In a bowl, combine the Ingredients.
2. Small servings are best served at a time.

Chicken & Yogurt

Ingredients

- 1 lb. chicken
- ½ lb. plain yogurt
- ½ can pumpkin puree
- ½ C. spinach

Directions

1. Cook the chicken until it's done to your liking.
2. Chop spinach.
3. Serve after combining all Ingredients.

Turkey Turmeric

Ingredients

- 1 lb. ground turkey
- Pinch of turmeric powder
- Pinch of ginger powder
- ½ C. plain yogurt

Directions

1. Fry the turkey in a pan.
2. Toss the turkey with turmeric and ginger.
3. Allow it cool, then stir in the yogurt before serving.

Tummy Medley

Ingredients

- ½ C. pumpkin puree
- ½ C. plain yogurt
- ½ C. banana
- Pinch of ginger

Directions

1. Mash or dice the bananas.
2. After combining all the Ingredients, serve in tiny portions.

Pumpkin Based Recipes

Pumpkin Mix

Ingredients

- 2 lb. chicken
- ½ C. pumpkin
- 1 can chickpeas
- C. cauliflower
- Tbsp. olive oil
- Optional eggs shells

Directions

1. Cook the chicken in a pot of boiling water until it is fully cooked through.
2. Chickpeas should be rinsed, drained, and then cooked in olive oil until soft and mashed.
3. Chop the cooked cauliflower finely after it has been steamed.
4. Combine all of the Ingredients in a large bowl.

Pumpkin & Squash

Ingredients

- 2 lb. chicken
- ¾ can pure natural pumpkin
- 1 yellow squash
- 1 C. rice
- Optional green pill, egg shells, or multivitamin

Directions

1. Cook the chicken in a pot of boiling water until it is done.
2. Cook the rice until it is tender, about 20 minutes.
3. Slice up steamed squash.
4. Mix the Ingredients together well.

Pumpkin Balls

Ingredients

- ½ C. pumpkin puree
- 1 C. coconut flour
- 1 C. quick-cooking oats

- 1 Tbsp. coconut oil
- 1 egg
- 1 eggshell
- 1 Tbsp. honey
- ¼ C. plain yogurt
- ¼ C. water

Directions

1. Preheat the oven to 350 degrees.
2. Bake the eggshell for seven minutes.
3. Pulverize the eggshells and oats together in a food processor until they are a fine powder.
4. Combine all of the Ingredients in a large bowl.
5. The mixture can be made into balls, or it can also be used to make muffins
6. Bake for around 15 minutes!

Pumpkin & Berry Oatmeal

Ingredients

- 2 C. steel-cut oats
- ¼ C. pumpkin puree
- ¼ C. blueberries
- ¼ C. chopped spinach

Directions

1. Soften the oats in a pot of water until they are mushy.
2. Remove stems from spinach leaves and chop finely
3. Stir together all of the Ingredients.
4. Serve!

Pumpkin Seeds & Turkey

Ingredients

- 2 C. pumpkin seeds
- 2 lb. of ground turkey
- Tbsp. olive oil

- 1 C. chopped cauliflower
- ½ C. chopped carrots

Directions

1. Prepare pumpkin seeds by boiling them for ten minutes.
2. Preheat your oven to 325 degrees.
3. Sprinkle olive oil on a baking sheet and bake pumpkin seeds for 10 minutes after patting them dry.
4. Carrots and cauliflower should be steamed before being chopped.
5. Stir together all of the Ingredients.

Peanut Butter & Chicken

Ingredients

- 2 lb. chicken
- 1 C. all-natural peanut butter
- Lb. carrots
- ½ lb. spinach
- Tbsp. coconut oil

Directions

1. Boil the chicken until it's tender and cooked through.
2. Steam the spinach and carrots until they are tender.
3. Peanut butter and coconut oil can be softened by melting them together (all-natural peanut butter is usually stickier)
4. Combine all items and stir well.

Sweet Potato & Peanut Butter

Ingredients

- sweet potatoes
- 1 C. white rice
- 1 C. all-natural peanut butter
- 1 apple, peeled and diced
- ½ C. carrots

Directions

1. Prepare the rice according to the package Directions until it's tender.
2. After puncturing the sweet potato, cook it in the microwave for ten minutes or until it is mushy.
3. Chop carrots after they've been steamed.
4. To soften peanut butter, heat it in the microwave.
5. Stir together all of the Ingredients.

Peanut Butter Oatmeal

Ingredients

- C. steel-cut oats
- 1 C. blueberries
- C. all-natural peanut butter
- Tbsp. coconut oil

Directions

1. Oats should be softened by cooking them.
2. Peanut butter and coconut oil should be heated in the microwave until they are less sticky.
3. Put everything together and serve!

Peanut Butter Banana Balls

Ingredients

- 1 banana
- 1⅔ C. quick-cooking oats
- ½ C. all-natural peanut butter
- ½ C. spinach, chopped
- ¼ C. all-natural honey

Directions

1. Fork the banana into a pulp.
2. Blend the spinach or slice it into tiny pieces.
3. Combine all Ingredients in a large bowl and thoroughly mix
4. Put in the freezer for approximately half an hour.
5. Shape into balls and store in the fridge.

Peanut Butter Mix

Ingredients

- lb. turkey
- 1 C. carrots
- 1 C. celery
- C. all-natural peanut butter
- ½ C. spinach
- Tbsp. coconut oil

Directions

1. Cook the turkey
2. Carrots and celery should be steamed and then chopped.
3. Chop spinach
4. Combine all Ingredients and serve.

Rosehip and Nettle Beef Stew

Ingredients

- 1lb. Beef
- ½ C. rice
- 1 ½ C. barley
- ½ C. lentils
- 2 C. chopped carrots
- 1 C. chopped celery
- 2 C. kale
- ½ C. dry seeded rosehips
- 1 C. fresh parsley
- 1 C. dry nettles

Directions

1. Add 8 C. of water to a saucepan, then add carrots and bring to a boil.
2. Toss the remainder of the Ingredients into the saucepan and bring it to a boil over medium heat.
3. Shut off the heat, cover the pot, and let it cool on its own.
4. Servings should be standard size.

Pumpkin Turmeric Treats

Ingredients

- 1 lb. Ground venison
- 1 C. oats
- 1 can organic pumpkin puree
- 75-100mg of turmeric per 5lb bodyweight
- 2 eggs
- 1 C. ground flax seed

Directions

1. Set the temperature of the oven to 250 degrees Fahrenheit and prepare the food.
2. Gather the Ingredients and mix them together.
3. Cut 45 pieces of dough out of it.
4. Bake for about three hours.
5. One goodie every day should be given.

Chicken Beef Patties

Ingredients

- 2 lb. Ground beef
- 2 lb. Ground chicken
- 1 apple without seeds
- eggs
- 2 carrots
- 2 C. raw goat milk
- 1 cubed zucchini

- 2 cubed sweet potatoes
- 2 C. kale

Directions

1. In a food processor, combine the Ingredients.
2. Separate the mixture into patties of appropriate sizes and freeze.
3. Defrost as necessary before feeding an animal.

Venison Meal

Ingredients

- 1lb. Ground venison
- 1 tbsp. Bone meal
- ½ C. organic plain yogurt
- 1 seeded, ribbed diced mild pepper
- 1 C. cooked brown rice
- 1 diced zucchini
- 1 tbsp. Ground flax seed
- 1 tsp. Olive oil
- ¼ C. diced red bell pepper
- 2 ½ C. water

Directions

1. Add the oil to a soup pot and bring it to a boil.
2. The venison should be cooked to a dark brown color.
3. Add zucchini, water, peppers
4. Cook for 20 minutes on the stovetop.
5. Remove from the heat and let it cool.
6. Stir in bone meal, flax seed, yogurt, and rice after it has cooled down.
7. Serve a normal-sized amount.

Orange Chicken

Ingredients

- 1 ½lb. Ground chicken

- 1 ½ tbsp. Bone meal
- ¼ lb. Broccoli florets
- 1 tangerine
- 1 seeded and mild ribbed pepper
- 1 diced sweet potato
- ¼ C. coconut oil
- ¼ lb. Chopped shiitake mushrooms
- ¼ lb. Diced zucchini
- 1 tbsp. Ground flax seed
- ¼ tsp. Rosemary
- ¼ tsp. Pepper
- ¼ tsp. Thyme

Directions

1. Add the meat, water, and spices to a pot and bring to a boil over medium-high heat, stirring often.
2. Boil for 20 minutes.
3. Add fruits and vegetables and cook until they are soft enough to pierce with a fork.
4. Take the pot off the stove and let it cool.
5. Add the flax seed, bone meal, and coconut oil.
6. Serve.

Tuna and Shrimp

Ingredients

- 1lb. Cooked shrimp ground finely
- 12 oz. Canned tuna in oil

- 1 cooked, mashed sweet potato
- ½ C. plain organic yogurt
- ¼ tsp. Black pepper
- ¼ tsp. Thyme
- ¼ tsp. Turmeric

Directions

1. Mix all the Ingredients in a large bowl to make patties.
2. Serve a standard portion for your dog.

Homemade Dog Food for Dogs with Diabetes

Chicken and Vegetable Meal

Ingredients

- 2 C. cooked chopped chicken breast
- 2 C. cooked long-grain brown rice
- ½ C. lightly steamed mixed vegetables
- ½ C. lightly steamed green beans
- ½ C. cottage cheese

Directions

1. Mix all the cooled Ingredients together in a large bowl
2. Serve a standard portion for your dog.

Chicken Stew

Ingredients

- Skinless, boneless chicken breast
- 1 C. pearl barley
- 1 ¾ lb. Diced tomatoes
- 1 lb. Fresh chopped green beans
- 1 lb. Chopped fresh broccoli and cauliflower mix
- C. water
- 2 tbsp. Olive oil

Directions

1. In a Dutch oven, mix the water and barley together.
2. Add chicken and olive oil to the mixture.
3. Cook the Ingredients for 40 minutes on low heat.
4. Remove the chicken to cool.
5. Cook the veggies until they are soft in the Dutch oven.
6. Chop the cooked chicken and mix it with the other Ingredients.
7. Allow it cool completely before slicing into regular serving sizes.
8. The leftover food may be frozen and defrosted as necessary.

Chuck and Barley Stew

Ingredients

- lb. Chopped chuck beef
- 1 lb. Pearl barley
- 2 lb. Chopped potatoes
- 2 lb. Chopped carrots
- ½ bunch celery, chopped
- 4 qt. water

Directions

1. Get a stockpot and add the meat, potatoes, celery, and carrots.
2. Add the water to the Ingredients.
3. Set a timer for one hour and cook at a high temperature.
4. The barley should be added to the boiling mixture after an hour.
5. Cook for a further 30 minutes.
6. Cool thoroughly before serving a routine-sized quantity.
7. Refrigerate or freeze leftover food and use it as required.

Beef and Cottage Cheese Meal

Ingredients

- ¼ lb. Ground lean beef
- 2 C. chopped fresh green beans
- 2 C. chopped fresh carrots
- ½ C. cottage cheese

Directions

1. Get a skillet and brown the beef. Pour away the fat.
2. Leave to cool.
3. Gently steam the carrots a d green beans in a pot of water.
4. Allow the vegetables to cool.
5. Mix all the Ingredients together.
6. Serve a portion appropriate for your dog.

Homemade Food for Dogs with Digestive Disorders

Chicken Casserole

Ingredients

- boneless, skinless chicken breasts
- C. low-sodium chicken broth
- ½ C. rolled oats
- ½ C. fresh chopped carrots
- ½ C. fresh chopped green beans
- ½ C. fresh chopped broccoli

Directions

1. Chop and slice the chicken breast into small pieces.
2. Get a skillet and cook the chicken.
3. Put the cooked chicken into a large saucepan and add the vegetables, chicken broth, and oats.
4. Cook the mixture on medium heat until the carrots are cooked enough but not mushy.
5. Allow it cool before serving
6. Store any leftovers in the refrigerator

Sweet Potato and Beef Stew

Ingredients

- 1lb. Cubed beef stew meat
- ½ C. fresh diced carrots
- 1 sweet potato
- ½ C. fresh diced green beans
- ½ C. all-purpose flour
- ½ C. water
- 1 tbsp. Vegetable oil

Directions

1. Let the sweet potato cool after baking.
2. If necessary, cut the stew meat into smaller pieces.
3. In a medium-sized pan, heat the vegetable oil over medium-high heat and add the stew meat.
4. Slice the sweet potato once it has been cooked.
5. Take the beef out of the pan and set it aside.
6. The flour and water should be added to the pan with the beef fat and stirred together. Keep stirring over low heat until a thick gravy develops.
7. Mix the beef and vegetables into the gravy.
8. Cook the veggies until they are easily pierced with a fork.
9. Let it cool down before serving a normal portion.
10. Keep any leftovers in the fridge.

Minced Chicken and Rice

Ingredients

- ½ C. ground chicken
- 1 C. white rice
- ¼ C. chopped carrots
- ¼ C. chopped green beans
- ½ tbsp. Corn oil
- ¼ tsp. Lite salt
- 1 tsp. Bone meal

Directions

1. Put water into a pot and heat it for the rice.
2. Pour the rice, corn oil, and salt into the boiling water.
3. Heat gently for 15 minutes.
4. Put the rest of the Ingredients into the pot and stir
5. Gently heat for 10 minutes
6. Remove the pot from the heat and allow the Ingredients to cool.
7. Serve and refrigerate any leftovers.

Chicken Neck Soup

Ingredients

- lb. Mixed chicken necks and chicken backs
- shiitake mushrooms
- 2 diced stalks of celery
- A handful of Italian parsley
- 2 diced carrots
- 1 grated knob of ginger
- 1 tbsp. Sea salt
- white peppercorns
- A dash of rosemary
- A dash of thyme

Directions

1. Put all the Ingredients into a large pot.

2. Heat the pot on high heat.

3. Remove the forming foam at the top of the pot, then heat gently.

4. Continue cooking for up to 8 hours

5. Leave to cool, then keep in the fridge overnight

6. Remove any fat from the top of the large pot

7. Pour out the broth and remove the solid contents

8. Serve the broth to your dog and refrigerate any leftovers.

Beef, Barley, and Broccoli

Ingredients

- ½ C. ground chicken
- 1 C. white rice
- ¼ C. chopped carrots
- ¼ C. chopped green beans
- ½ tbsp. Corn oil
- ¼ tsp. Lite salt
- 1 tsp. Bone meal

Directions

1. Prepare the barley by following the instructions on the package.

2. Slice the stew beef into little pieces.

3. Put the beef in a skillet and cook it until done

4. Steam the zucchini and broccoli gently.

5. After steaming, mash the broccoli and zucchini together

6. Allow the Ingredients to cool, then mix them together

7. Serve an appropriate amount for your dog and refrigerate the leftovers

Chicken and Rice

Ingredients

- 2 C. low-sodium chicken stock or bone broth
- 1 C. cooked, diced chicken
- 1 C. white rice

- 2 C. water

Directions

1. Mix the Ingredients together in a large saucepan.
2. Heat on high heat until boiling.
3. Cover the saucepan, then reduce the heat. Continue to heat until the rice is fluffy.
4. Allow it cool before serving.
5. Refrigerate any leftovers.

Tapioca and Tofu

Ingredients

- 10.5 oz. Plain tofu
- C. tapioca
- ¼ tsp. Salt
- Potassium chloride (amount depends on the weight of your dog)

Directions

1. Tapioca should be cooked as directed on the box, using salt and potassium chloride in water to prevent the starch from sticking.
2. Allow the tapioca to cool completely.
3. Finely chop the tofu and mix it with the tapioca that has been left to cool.
4. Add calcium carbonate to the mixture.
5. Serve a normal-sized portion. Keep any leftovers in the fridge.

Beef in the Slow Cooker

Ingredients

- 2 ½ lb. Lean ground beef
- 15 oz. Can dark red kidney beans, be drained and rinsed
- 1 ½ C. brown rice
- 1 ½ C. diced carrots
- 1 ½ C. diced squash
- ½ C. garden peas
- C. water

Directions

1. Put all the Ingredients into a Crockpot and close the lid
2. Cook on low heat for six hours while stirring from time to time.
3. Put off the heat and leave to cool.
4. Serve and put any leftovers in the fridge for storage.

Chicken, Eggs, and Rice

Ingredients

- 1 C. boiled chopped chicken
- 1 hardboiled egg, chopped
- 2 tbsp. Organic non-fat plain yogurt
- ¼ C. cooked brown rice
- ½ C. lightly steamed Peas and Carrots

Directions

1. Mix all the cooked Ingredients and stir well to mix.
2. Leave to cool, then serve.
3. Store any leftovers in the refrigerator.

Homemade Dog Food Recipes for Dogs having Kidney disease

Beef and Tofu

Ingredients

- 1 lb. Of boiled Low-fat ground beef
- ½ oz. Plain tofu
- 2 C. cooked white rice
- 1 C. cottage cheese
- 2 C. lightly steamed, sliced carrots
- ½ C. wheat bran
- 1 capsule of flaxseed oil

Directions

1. Slice the tofu into tiny pieces
2. Leave the cooked Ingredients to cool
3. Mix the Ingredients together and serve
4. Store the leftovers in the refrigerator

Homemade Dog Food Recipes for Dogs having live disorders

Beef and Brown Rice Dinner

Ingredients

- 1/8 lb ground beef
- 1 egg
- 1 1/3 C. brown rice
- 1 carrot, grated
- 1 minced clove
- Liquid vitamin B (amount depends on the weight of your dog)
- Calcium powder (amount depends on the weight of your dog)
- Multivitamin (amount depends on the weight of your dog)

Directions

1. Follow the instructions on the rice packaging and cook the rice.
2. Mix the eggs and ground beef
3. Allow the rice to cool before mixing it 2ith the beef and egg mixture. Stir well to mix.
4. Mix the calcium powder, vitamin B, and multivitamin together.
5. Add the vitamin and calcium mixture to the rice mixture. Stir well to mix.
6. Serve an appropriate size for your dog.
7. Refrigerate the leftovers.

White Rice and Beef

Ingredients

- ¼ lb. Ground beef

- 2 C. cooked white rice
- 1 hardboiled egg, chopped
- slices of white bread, Shredded into small pieces
- Calcium carbonate (amount depends on the weight of your dog)

Directions

1. Get a skillet and brown the beef in it.
2. Leave the beef to cool.
3. Put the other Ingredients into the beef. Stir well to mix.
4. Serve an appropriate size for your dog, and refrigerate any remaining.

Homemade Dog Food for Improving Skin and Coat Health

Peanut Butter and Fish Oil Treats

Ingredients

- 1 C. oats
- 2 C. whole wheat flour
- 1 tbsp. Honey
- 1/3 C. all-natural peanut butter
- ½ tbsp. Salmon oil
- 1 ½ C. water

Directions

1. Prepare the oven by preheating it to 350 degrees.
2. Mix a C. of water with all the Ingredients and stir well to mix.
3. If needed, add more water to get a cookie-like dough.
4. Roll the dough to get ¼" thickness.
5. Cut the dough using a 1" cookie cutter.
6. Place on a cookie sheet and bake the cookie shape dough in the oven for 49 minutes.
7. Leave to cool.
8. Treat your dog once a day.

Homemade Dog Food for Increasing Weight

Chicken, Beef, and Oats

Ingredients

- 1lb. Ground beef
- 2 chicken leg quarters
- 1 C. brown rice
- 2/3 C. oats
- 1 C. cottage cheese
- 2 grated carrots
- 14 Oz. Can dark red kidney beans be rinsed, drained, and mashed
- 2 C. chopped frozen broccoli
- 1 large bag of frozen spinach
- 1 minced clove
- ½ C. olive oil

Directions

1. Place the chicken quarters in a big pot, and then pour water over them until they reach the chicken's top by a single inch.
2. Put the chicken pan on the stove and bring the water to a boil.
3. When the chicken is well cooked, lower the heat to a simmer, cover the pan, and simmer for 40 minutes.
4. Take out the chicken and let it cool.
5. After straining the chicken water to remove any leftover particles, put it back on the stove.
6. The rice, veggies, and beans should all be added to the water, and then bring the pot to a boil.
7. While the mixture is heating, place the beef in a skillet and cook.
8. Reduce the heat on the mixture to a simmer and continue to cook until the vegetables are tender to touch with a fork.
9. Empty the grease from the beef and place it into a large mixing bowl.
10. Remove the meat from the chicken. Add it to the large mixing bowl containing the beef.
11. When the bean mixture is cooked enough, leave it to cool.
12. Mix the meets with the bean mixture and the rest of the Ingredients.
13. Serve and store any leftovers in the refrigerator.

Homemade Low-fat" Dog Food Recipes

Homemade Beef Dinner

Ingredients

- 5 lb. of ground beef (cut the fat)
- 2.5 C. cooked brown rice (or oatmeal, lentils, oatmeal, or quinoa)
- 3 C. of mixed vegetables

Directions

1. Begin by cooking all the Ingredients together, leaving out the vegetables. Add the vegetables for a few minutes before the meat is done.

Homemade Chicken Dinner

- 5 lb. of chicken (cut the fat)
- 2 C. of red cabbage
- 2 skinned apples
- 2 C. of spinach
- 5 cooked eggs
- 2 Tbsp. of olive oil

Directions

1. The Ingredients can all be cooked together or mixed together raw if the meat has bones

Ground Beef Recipe

Ingredients

- 1 C. of lean ground beef
- ½ C. of the beef kidney (trim the fat)
- 1/4 C. kale
- ½ C. yellow crookneck squash
- 1 C. of uncooked oatmeal

Directions

1. boil the Ingredients separately, then mix them
2. then add the uncooked oatmeal
3. serve

Doggie low-fat dessert

Ingredients

- 2 lb. of chopped-up cooked chicken (cut the fat)
- 3 C. of mixed fruit
- 3 C. of cooked brown rice (or lentils, oatmeal, or quinoa)

Directions

1. Mix all the Ingredients together

Homemade Fish Dinner

Ingredients

- 2 lb. of fish fillets
- 1 or 2 cans of pink salmon
- 3 C. of diced vegetables
- 1 C. of cooked brown rice (or quinoa, oatmeal, or lentils)

Directions

1. Prepare the fish and vegetables by cooking them.
2. Mix them and allow them to cool
3. serve

Doggie Chili

Ingredients

- 4 cooked chicken breasts (remove the fat)
- 1 C. of drained kidney beans
- 1 C. of drained black beans
- 1 C. of carrots
- ½ C. of tomato paste
- 4 C. of chicken broth

Directions

1. Mix all the Ingredients together and cook them for 10 minutes
2. Serve

Mixed Meat Goodness

Ingredients

- 3 lb. of cooked whole wheat macaroni
- 2 lb. of chicken thighs (remove fat)
- 1 lb. of lean ground beef
- 1 lb. broccoli stalks
- 1 lb. red leaf lettuce
- ½ lb. chicken liver
- ½ lb. beef heart
- Egg white from 1 large egg
- 4 Tbsp. of eggshell powder
- 1 Tbsp. of kelp meal
- 10+ drops of vitamin E

Directions

1. Cook the Ingredients together. Add the vegetables for 10 minutes until the meat is done
2. Serve

Cheesy Beef with Rice

Ingredients

- 1 C. cooked lean ground beef (remove the fat)
- 1 C. cooked brown rice
- 1 C. non-fat cheese
- ½ C. cooked broccoli
- ½ C. cooked squash

Directions

1. Cook each ingredient separately
2. Cook separately and then mix.

Chicken with Broccoli and Rice

Ingredients

- 5 lb. diced chicken (cut the fat)
- 5 C. cooked brown rice or oatmeal, lentils or quinoa
- 3 C. chopped broccoli
- 3 Tbsp. of olive oil

Directions

1. Cook each meat separately.
2. Mix the meats, then finish by adding the broccoli

3. Serve

Raw Chicken Dinner

Ingredients

- 6 oz. chicken necks and thighs
- 1 lb. baked sweet potato
- ½ lb. of broccoli stalks
- 3 oz. of chicken liver
- 1/4 Tbsp. of iodized salt
- 2 to 5 drops of vitamin E

Directions

1. Cook all the Ingredients together. Then add the vegetables at the last 10 minutes of cooking the meat.
2. Serve

Homemade Hypoallergenic Dog Food Recipes

Basic Chicken plus Rice recipe

Ingredients

- 4 chicken breasts
- 2 C. of chopped vegetables (for instance, broccoli or cauliflower)
- ½ C. of brown rice
- 3 C. of chicken broth

Directions

1. Cook all the Ingredients together. Then add the vegetables at the last 10 minutes of cooking the meat.
2. Serve

Sweet Chicken

Ingredients

- 2 lb. chicken
- 1 C. of red cabbage
- 1 skinned apple

- 1 C. of spinach
- 2 cooked eggs
- 1 Tbsp. of olive oil

Directions

1. The food can be mixed and served raw if the chicken has bones.

Chicken and Potato Recipe

Ingredients

- ½ C. of cooked chicken breast
- 6 C. of boiled potatoes
- 4 Tbsp. chicken fat
- 3 calcium carbonate tablets
- 1 multiple vitamin-mineral tablets

Directions

1. Cook all the Ingredients together. Then add the vegetables at the last 10 minutes of cooking the meat.
2. Serve

Turkey With Veggies

Ingredients

- 2 lb. of turkey meat
- 2 C. of cooked brown rice
- 1 C. of green beans
- 1 C. of carrots
- ½ C. of water
- 2 Tbsp. vegetable oil

Directions

1. Cook all the Ingredients together. Then add the vegetables at the last 10 minutes of cooking the meat.
2. Serve

Eggs and Cheese Mild Homemade Recipe

Ingredients

- 6 scrambled eggs
- ½ C. of cottage cheese
- 1 C. of cooked brown rice

Directions

1. Mix all the Ingredients together.
2. Cook the mixed Ingredients and serve

Fish-Veggie Patty

Ingredients

- 2 cans of Salmon
- 2 potatoes
- 2 carrots
- 2 cooked eggs
- 2 stalks of celery
- 5 Tbsp. of flour

Directions

1. Drain the salmon, then fry with the egg and flour
2. After removing them from the oil then, add the vegetables
3. Mix them and leave to cool
4. Serve

Homemade Kibble Recipe

Ingredients

- 4 beaten eggs
- ½ C. olive oil
- 1 C. of cooked cream whole wheat

Directions

1. Mix the Ingredients and spread evenly on a baking sheet
2. place in the oven to bake for 50 minutes
3. Take out of the oven and allow to cool, then place in the refrigerator to freeze.
4. Bring out thaw, and serve.

Ground Round Dog Food

Ingredients

- 2 lb. ground round meat, sautéed in olive oil
- 1 C. cooked brown rice
- 4 boiled eggs
- 1 package of cauliflower
- 1 package of chopped carrots
- 4 Tbsp. of low-fat cottage cheese
- 2 Tbsp. of bone meal

Directions

1. Cook the Ingredients together, then add the vegetables in the last 10 minutes before the meat is done.
2. Serve

Cheese and Chicken Dinner

Ingredients

- 3 C. cooked chicken meat (remove the fat)
- 3 C. cooked brown rice (or oatmeal, quinoa, or lentils)
- 3 C. cream cheese
- 1.5 C. of cooked broccoli
- 1.5 C. of cooked squash

Direction

1. Cook the Ingredients together, then add the vegetables in the last 10 minutes before the meat is done.
2. Serve

Doggie Peanut Butter Delight

Ingredients

- 1.5 of water
- 1/4 C. of oil
- 3 eggs
- 3 Tbsp. of peanut butter
- 2 Tbsp. of vanilla
- 2 C. of whole wheat flour
- ½ C. of cornflour
- ½ C. of oats

Directions

1. Mix the Ingredients and form the dough.
2. Roll the dough and cut un cookie-sized pieces.
3. Place in the oven and bake for 20 minutes.

Dog Food Recipes for Senior Dogs

Doggie's Stew

Ingredients

- 5 lb. boneless chicken breasts and thighs
- 5 oz. chicken livers
- 5 oz. chicken gizzards
- 5 lb. carrots
- 1 lb. green beans
- ½ lb. pumpkin
- .5-1 lb. apples
- 1-2 big sweet potatoes

Directions

1. Cook the Ingredients together at a temperature of 250 degrees
2. after cooking, blend with a hand blender
3. serve

Scaled-down Doggie's Stew

Ingredients

- 2 lb. boneless chicken breasts and thighs
- 1 lb. catfish
- 1/4 lb. chicken livers and/or gizzards
- ½ lb. carrots
- ½ oz. green beans
- ½ C. pumpkin
- 1 apple
- 1 small sweet potato

Directions

1. Cook the Ingredients together at a temperature of 250 degrees.
2. After cooking, blend with a hand blender.
3. Serve.

Chili Goodness

Ingredients

- 2 cooked chicken breasts
- ½ C. drained kidney beans
- ½ C. drained black beans
- 1/4 of a C. tomato paste
- ½ C. carrots
- 2 C. chicken broth

Directions

1. Mix all the Ingredients and cook the mixture for 10 minutes

Chicken Soup Cookies

Ingredients

- 1 C. ground high-quality dry dog food kibble
- 2 C. Bisquick baking mix

- 1 18.8 oz. can of chicken soup

Directions

1. Mix the Ingredients and place the mixture on cookie sheets.
2. Bake until done.
3. Serve

Beef Delight

Ingredients

- 2 lb. of ground beef
- 1 C. of cooked brown rice
- 1 and a half C. mixed vegetables

Directions

1. Cook the Ingredients together, then add the vegetables in the last 10 minutes before the meat is done.
2. Serve

Veggies and Chicken

- 2 lb. of chicken
- 2 C. of cooked rice
- 1 C. of chopped broccoli
- 1 Tbsp. of olive oil

Directions

1. Cook the Ingredients together, then add the vegetables in the last 10 minutes before the meat is done.
2. Serve

Frosty Paws

Ingredients

- 32 oz. of vanilla yogurt
- 1 large mashed banana
- 2 Tbsp. of peanut butter
- 2 Tbsp. of honey

Directions

1. Blend all the Ingredients in a blender and freeze in little quantities.

Oldie but Goldie

Ingredients

- 2 C. of ground chicken meat
- ½ C. of chicken liver
- 1 C. of cooked rice
- ½ C. of vegetables
- 2 cooked eggs
- 1 Tbsp. of fish oil

Directions

1. Cook the Ingredients together, then add the vegetables in the last 10 minutes before the meat is done.
2. Serve

Raw Fish Delight

Ingredients

- 4 lb. of fish fillets
- 2 cans of pink salmon
- 3 eggs
- 4 Tbsp. of oregano
- 8 Tbsp. of parsley
- 1 C. of cooked brown rice

Directions

1. Mix all the Ingredients together
2. Serve

Homemade Breakfast for Dogs

Egg Breakfast of Champions

Ingredients

- One or Two Eggs
- 5-10 baby spinach leaves
- Sprinkle of dried Kelp

Directions

1. begin by frying the eggs
2. chop the spinach
3. Remove the egg and allow it to cool
4. fry the spinach for about 15 seconds, then add it to the eggs
5. sprinkle a little kelp on the eggs
6. serve!

Home-Made Dinner for Dogs

Chicken, Broccoli & Rice Dinner

Ingredients

- 5 lb. of diced chicken
- 5 whole eggs, raw or cooked
- 5 C. of white or brown rice
- 3 C. of broccoli, chopped
- 3 Tbsp. of olive oil

Directions

1. Boil the rice and chicken together until the chicken is just cooked
2. Put in the broccoli and reduce the heat to simmer until the chicken is done
3. Serve and Put in any leftovers in the refrigerator

Beef Balls Dinner for Dogs

Ingredients

- 10 lb. of ground beef
- 10 whole eggs, raw or cooked
- 5 C. rice or lentils
- 3 C. of mixed vegetables

Directions

1. Put the rice or lentils in a pot of water with the meat and cook. Add the vegetables just when the meat is about to be done.
2. Allow the mixture to cool, then mix them up and roll them into meatballs
3. Serve

Homemade Raw Food for Dogs

Grain-Free Raw Dog Food

Ingredients

- 60% Meat
- 25% Vegetables
- 5% Organ Meats: liver or hearts
- 10% Other – Any from Eggs, Plain Yogurt,
- Fish or Krill, Flax, Kefir, Oil, Coconut
- Daily Supplements
- 1/8 tsp Bone Meal: per 15 lbs body weight
- Any additional vitamins or supplements per

Directions

1. Grind or chop the vegetables or meat, then mix
2. Separate into meal portions.
3. Serve and refrigerate any remaining portions

Meaty Homemade Dog Food

Slow-Cooked Canine Chicken

Ingredients

- 1 C. uncooked brown rice
- 3 boneless, skinless chicken breasts
- 2 carrots, cut into 1 round
- 1 sweet potato, cubed (unpeeled but with all the green parts removed)
- ½ C. cranberries Water, as needed

Directions

1. Pour water into a 4-quart or larger slow cooker, then add the rest of the Ingredients and seal the lid.
2. Cook on low for at least 12 hours, up to overnight.
3. Before serving or refrigerating, allow the dish to cool.

Raw Chicken Dinner

Ingredients

- 1 lb. raw chicken, chopped
- 2 whole chicken livers, rinsed and chopped
- 1 egg
- ½ clove , chopped (optional)
- 2 Tbsp. low-fat plain yogurt
- 1 tsp. raw honey
- 1 Tbsp. organic apple cider vinegar
- ½ tsp. flaxseed oil
- 1 tsp. kelp seaweed powder

- 1 tsp. alfalfa powder

Directions

1. Get a large bowl and mix all the Ingredients using a spoon.
2. Refrigerate for 3 days
3. Serve a meal-sized portion to your dog and refrigerate any leftovers.

Salmon Balls

Ingredients

- 1½ C. cooked salmon, chopped
- 1 egg
- 1 C. of brown rice
- 1 Tbsp. olive oil

Directions

1. Pre-heat the oven to 350°F.
2. Clean and prepare a baking sheet by spraying with non-stick cooking spray or lining it with parchment paper.
3. Get a bowl of medium size a mix all of the Ingredients completely.
4. To make the balls, scoop the mixture using a spoon or melon baller and roll each one into a ball.
5. Spread out on a baking sheet.
6. Bake for about 15 minutes.
7. Before serving or storing, allow desserts to cool completely.

Sardine Cakes

Ingredients

- Cakes (based on the size of the sweet potatoes)
- 2 cooked sweet potatoes
- 2 cans of sardines in water (drained and chopped)
- 1 clove of , crushed (optional)
- 1 egg, beaten
- 2 Tbsp. all-purpose flour
- 1½ C. panko bread crumbs, divided

- Olive oil, as needed

Directions

1. Peel sweet potato skins and mash potatoes in a big dish.
2. Mix in the sardines, , egg, and flour.
3. Add 1 C. of bread crumbs and thoroughly combine.
4. Create little 3" patties out of the mixture.
5. Roll the patties in the leftover bread crumbs.
6. In a large pan, heat approximately 2 Tbsp. of olive oil over medium-high heat.
7. Two or three sardine patties should be fried at a time for 5-8 minutes, turning once throughout that time, till golden brown.
8. Prior to offering to your dog, drain on a paper towel and let it cool fully.

Beef Fried Rice

Ingredients

- 2 C. water
- 1 C. uncooked jasmine rice
- 2 eggs
- 1 lb. lean ground beef
- ½ C. sliced celery
- ½ C. low-sodium soy sauce
- 1 Tbsp. sesame oil
- ½ C. frozen chopped carrots and peas

Directions

1. Heat water on high in a saucepan.
2. Put in the rice as the water is boiling.
3. Continue heating, then reduce the heat and simmer until the rice is soft for about 20-25 minutes.
4. Use a non-stick cooking spray to spray a large skillet and heat it on medium heat.
5. Beat eggs and add into a skillet, and heat until firm.
6. Leave the egg to cool and slice it into strips.
7. Mix the rice and eggs and keep them to the side. Place the skillet on the stove.
8. Cook the celery and beef on medium heat for 10 minutes or until the picture is cooked. Stir from time to time to prevent overbrowning.

9. Mix the sesame oil and soy sauce, then add the beef to the mixture.
10. Add the cooked rice, carrot, cooked egg strips, and carrot. Stir from time to time for 3-4 minutes to mix well.
11. Allow it to cool before serving.

Terrier's Tuna Casserole

Ingredients

- 1 can tuna packed in water
- 1 C. cooked pasta, drained
- ½ C. frozen peas, thawed
- ¼ C. chopped fresh parsley
- ¼ C. grated Parmesan cheese

Directions

1. When you're done draining the tuna, save the water and use it in a treat recipe instead of regular water.
2. Mix tuna, pasta, peas, parsley, and cheese in a medium bowl.
3. Serve.
4. Keep any leftovers in the refrigerator.
5. You can keep it safe in an airtight jar at room temperature for up to three months.

Chicken and Rice Tender Tummy Meal

Ingredients

- 2 chicken breasts
- 2 qt. water
- 1 C. white rice

Directions

1. Chicken breasts should have their bones, fat, and skin removed and disposed of.
2. Put water into a large pot. Heat the pot of water on medium heat until it boils.
3. Add chicken breasts and heat until the flesh is no longer pink in the middle.
4. The chicken should be removed from the water after it's done cooking; add rice to the water and reduce the heat to medium-low to cook.
5. Take care not to overcook your rice (at least 30 minutes).
6. Take it off the heat so it can cool down and soak up more water.

7. After 30 minutes, drain off any remaining water but keep the soup wet and somewhat soupy.
8. With a pair of forks, shred the chicken while the rice is simmering.
9. Return the chicken to the pot with the rice after it has finished cooking and allow it to cool fully. Serve.
10. Store the food in a container that is airtight for up to six months.

Stuffed Pumpkin

Ingredients

- 1 (3-lb.) cooking pumpkin
- 1 apple
- 1 C. green beans, cooked
- ½ lb. ground turkey or ground chicken
- 2 Tbsp. grated Parmesan cheese

Directions

1. Preheat the oven to 350°F.
2. Use a spoon to scoop out the pumpkin's insides to remove the seeds.
3. (Reserve the seeds for later use.)
4. Get the Pumpkin and remove the seeds and core and then finely slice the fruit.
5. Slice the green beans.
6. Combine the green beans, apple, turkey, and Parmesan cheese in a medium bowl and mix well. Stuff pumpkin with the mixture. Bake a pumpkin on a baking sheet in the center of the oven for one hour.
7. During the cooking process, be sure to drain any liquid that has accumulated on the top of the pumpkin.
8. Before serving, allow the food to cool fully.
9. In order to serve, halve the pumpkin before cutting it in half.
10. Scoop out the food from the pumpkin, including the flesh.
11. Unused portions may be kept in the refrigerator for up to three days or frozen for up to two months.

Salmon and Spinach Hash

Ingredients

- 1 tsp. olive oil
- 1 (7.5-oz.) can salmon, drained
- 1 C. frozen spinach, thawed

- Eggs

Directions

1. Pour the olive oil into a medium-sized pan and heat over medium heat.
2. Stir in the fish and spinach until cooked through.
3. The eggs should be scrambled and then added to the pan.
4. Allow it to cool, then serve. Store for up to 3 days in the refrigerator.

Lamb Hash

Ingredients

- 2 Tbsp. olive oil
- 1 lb. ground lamb
- 1 C. frozen mixed vegetables (without onions)
- 2 C. cooked brown rice
- 2 C. cooked white rice
- 1 C. low-fat plain yogurt

Directions

1. Oil may be heated in a big pan over high heat.
2. Cook the lamb for approximately 10 minutes until it's no longer pink and drain the fat.
3. Defrost the veggies by stirring them in.
4. Take off the heat.
5. Mix the rice and yogurt with the lamb mixture in a large bowl.
6. Mix thoroughly.
7. Before serving, let the food cool down.
8. To get the best results, store it in the refrigerator, where it can last for up to three days

Buffalo Meatballs

Ingredients

- 2 slices whole-wheat bread, cut into ½" cubes
- ½ C. milk
- 1 egg
- 1/3 C. grated Parmesan cheese
- 2 Tbsp. finely chopped parsley

- 1 lb. ground bison
- Olive oil, for frying

Directions

1. Pour milk into a medium-sized bowl and soak bread cubes until they're pliable (about 5 minutes).
2. Using a bread masher, remove the bread from the milk, and discard the remaining milk.
3. Mix the bread, egg, cheese, parsley, and bison in a large bowl.
4. Roll little bits into balls by pinching them off with your fingers and rolling them in your hands.
5. 12 C. of olive oil should be heated in a large pan over medium-high heat.
6. The meatballs should be fried until they are no longer pink in the middle, around 8–10 minutes.
7. Before serving, allow the food to cool fully.
8. Store in an airtight jar in the refrigerator for 3–4 days or freeze for up to 6 months.

Turkey Kibble

Ingredients

- 2 lb. of kibble
- ½ C. whole-wheat flour
- 2 C. non-fat dry milk powder
- 2 eggs
- ½ C. extra-virgin olive oil
- 1 lb. uncooked lean ground turkey

Direction

1. 2 C. puréed, cooked sweet potato without skin (or try substituting pumpkin, green beans, or a mix)
2. Preheat the oven to 200°F.
3. Set aside a cookie sheet that has been lightly oiled.
4. Mix flour, dry milk powder, eggs, and olive oil in a large bowl.
5. Mix in the ground turkey and the pureed vegetables.
6. Mix well.
7. Using a lightly floured board, roll out the dough to a thickness of 14 - 12".
8. Transfer the cookie batter to a baking sheet.
9. To make kibble, use a pizza cutter to cut the dough into the desired size.
10. Bake for 90 minutes.
11. Put off the oven and allow the kibble cool to room temperature and firm before serving.

12. Remove the kibble from the oven after it's cooled and break it into pieces along the score lines.
13. Put in a bag and store in the fridge for about three days.

Chicken and Sardine Kibble

Ingredients

- 3 sweet potatoes, baked
- 1½ C. water, divided
- 1 lb. cooked chicken gizzards
- Sardines in water in a can
- ½ C. whole-wheat flour
- 2 C. non-fat dry milk powder
- 3 eggs
- ¾ C. extra-virgin olive oil

Directions

1. Begin the recipe by preheating the oven to 250 °F.
2. Two baking sheets should be lightly oiled.
3. Peel and discard the skins of sweet potatoes.
4. Blend or puree sweet potatoes with ½ C. water in a blender or food processor until smooth.
5. Set away for a later time.
6. Blend or grind gizzards with ½ cup water to a fine powder, then blend in the sardines until they are smooth.
7. Mix the flour, milk powder, eggs, and olive oil in a large bowl until smooth.
8. Mix in puréed sweet potato, chopped gizzards, and chopped sardines.
9. Spread the dough evenly on a lightly floured surface.
10. Add more flour as needed. After bringing the dough to a uniform consistency, it should be rolled out to a thickness of 14–12
11. Using a pizza cutter, cut strips and set them on cookie sheets.
12. The distance between the strips on the cookie sheets should be at least ½ inch.
13. After 45 minutes of baking, the strips should be turned over.
14. Based on the size of your dog, cut the strips into ½" squares using a pizza cutter. Then again bake the cookie sheets for another 45 minutes before turning off the oven.
15. Flip all of the squares with a spatula, being careful not to make any contact.

16. Alternatively, if you have a second batch of kibble that has to be baked, transfer the kibble to drying racks for cooling.
17. After cooling, put one week's worth of kibble in the refrigerator; the rest can be frozen for up to 6 months.

Substituting Flour

In a situation where your dog is allergic to wheat, you may easily substitute rice, buckwheat, and so on for wheat flour in your recipes.

Because wheat flour contains gluten, which gives baked foods their springy texture, you'll need to employ a thickening agent like guar gum (which is also present in many commercial wet dog food products).

Buffalo Hash

Ingredients

- 2 Tbsp. olive oil
- 1 lb. ground buffalo
- 2 eggs
- 2 C. frozen chopped vegetables (without onion)
- 2 C. cooked brown rice

Directions

1. Using a big pan, heat the olive oil until it is hot but not smoking.
2. Stir in the ground buffalo and cook for approximately 10 minutes, or until the buffalo no longer appears pink.
3. Bring down the heat to medium and put in the eggs, chopped veggies, and brown rice after draining the fat.
4. Cook the eggs, occasionally stirring, until they are set.
5. Allow to cool to room temperature before serving or storing.
6. To store for a longer time, keep in the refrigerator for 3 days or store in an airtight container for up to 6 months

Chicken Meatloaf

Ingredients

- ½ C. barley
- 4 C. Homemade Chicken Broth
- 1½ lb. ground chicken
- ½ C. low-fat cottage cheese
- 2 whole eggs

- ½ C. of rolled oats ¾ C. of finely chopped carrots
- 1 Tbsp. olive oil

Directions

1. The barley and chicken broth should be brought to boil in a medium saucepan, then reduce the heat and simmer for forty-five minutes.
2. Put away to cool.
3. The oven should be preheated to 350 °F.
4. Use a non-stick cooking spray to spray a 9-by-13-inch baking dish.
5. Gather all of the Ingredients for the meatloaf together in a large bowl.
6. Mix well.
7. Stir in the broth and barley gradually.
8. Make sure everything is mixed completely.
9. Put the resulting mixture into the prepared pan and bake for 1 hour.

Veggie Substitutes

Instead of carrots, you can also use other veggies in this meatloaf:

Mutt Meatloaf Meal

Ingredients

- 4 lb. lean ground turkey
- ½ lb. organic beef liver or chicken liver, rinsed and diced
- 4 eggs
- 2 C. puréed carrots, steamed
- 2 C. puréed potatoes, steamed
- 2 C. puréed green beans, steamed

Directions

1. Preheat the oven you want to use to 350°F before beginning.
2. Make four 8" x 4" x 212" loaf pans by combining all of the Ingredients.
3. Each loaf pan should be roughly three-quarters filled.
4. Leave to bake for 1 hour.
5. Drain the fat from the pan.
6. Cool and serve then and place one week's worth of food in the refrigerator

7. If you have leftover meatloaf, wrap it in foil or put it in a zip-top bag and store it in a freezer for up to six months.

More Meatloaf Options

You can prepare this recipe with ground chicken, ground lamb, or ground beef.

There are many more options, such as broccoli (with the stems), as well as sweet potatoes, and cauliflower.

Raw Meatloaf

Ingredients

- 1 lb. raw ground beef, bison, lamb, turkey, or chicken
- 2 C. puréed vegetables
- ¼ C. liver, gizzards, or kidneys, rinsed
- ½ C. organic apple cider vinegar
- ½ C. low-fat plain yogurt
- 3 eggs with shells, finely broken

Directions

1. Get a large bowl, mix the Ingredients thoroughly in a large bowl and stir well.
2. To store for a longer time, keep in the refrigerator for three days or store in an airtight container for up to 6 months

---

Raw Power Homemade Dog Food Recipes

Spot's Spinach and Sprats

Ingredients

- 2 Tbsp. olive oil
- 2 C. cooked brown rice, chilled
- 2 loose C. fresh spinach, chopped
- 1 (8.5-oz.) can sprats, drained and chopped

Directions

1. Apply non-stick spray to a big skillet.
2. Use a fork to whip the eggs in a small bowl
3. In a pan, place the eggs and cook them over medium heat until they've set.

4. Removing the pan from the heat.
5. Transfer the eggs from the pan and slice them into long pieces.
6. Return the skillet to the stove over medium heat and add olive oil.
7. Toss in the rice and spinach in the pan and cook for a minute or two, then remove from heat.
8. When the spinach wilts, remove it from the heat.
9. Then add the sprats and the eggs and mix until everything is well-combined.
10. Allow it to cool before serving.
11. To store for a longer time, keep in the refrigerator for three days or store in an airtight container for up to 6 months

Mini Liver Quiche

Ingredients

- ¼ lb. chicken livers, rinsed and cooked 3 eggs
- ¼ C. diced, cooked green beans
- The oven should be preheated at 350 °F.

Directions

1. Prepare the muffin tins by greasing them or lining them with paper cup. Crush the chicken livers with the back of a fork and cut any bigger pieces into smaller pieces.
2. In a medium bowl, whisk the eggs before adding the chicken livers and green beans and folding them together.
3. After filling muffin pans three-quarters of the way with the mixture, bake the muffins in the oven until they are golden brown, which should take around thirty minutes but might vary depending on the size of the muffins.
4. To store for a longer time, keep in the refrigerator for three days or store in an airtight container for up to 6 months

Baked Egg Cup

Ingredients

- ½ C. cottage cheese
- ½ tsp. baking powder
- 1 C. shredded Cheddar cheese
- ½ C. shredded cooked chicken
- 1 (5-oz.) can tuna in water, drained

Directions

1. Preheat the oven to 350°F.
2. Prepare a mini-muffin tin by lining the C. with parchment paper.
3. Into a large mixing bowl, beat the eggs, and then stir in the yogurt, cottage cheese, baking powder, cheese, chicken, and tuna.
4. Pour the mixture of the egg into separate C. until it is about two-thirds full.
5. Bake for about 30 minutes.
6. Wait until it's cool to serve.
7. To store for a longer time, keep in the refrigerator for three days

Chia Seed Oatmeal

Ingredients

- 1 C. unsweetened almond milk
- 1 C. old-fashioned oats
- 2 Tbsp. chia seeds
- 2 apples
- 2 Tbsp. raw honey
- 1 tsp. lemon juice
- 1 C. plain or Greek yogurt with no added sugar

Directions

1. Fill up a medium bowl with oats and chia seeds, then add almond milk.
2. Set it apart.
3. The apples should be peeled, cored, and grated before being tossed with honey and lemon juice. (Don't forget to remove the apple seeds.)
4. Mix chopped apples and yogurt into the bowl of chia seeds and oats.
5. Stir to mix well, cover, and refrigerate overnight.
6. Chill the chia seed mixture for at least 12 hours before serving so that the seeds can expand.
7. Refrigerate for a maximum of five days.
8. Wake Up to Chia
9. Chia seeds have been around since the time of the Aztecs and Mayans, but they were made known to the general public by Chia Pets, which were terracotta figures that were famous in the 1980s because they sprouted chia "foliage" and "fur."

10. There are few whole foods that can compete with the antioxidant power of chia seeds today in terms of nutrient content and other health benefits.

Spinach Omelet

Ingredients

- 1 omelet 2 eggs
- 1 C. baby spinach leaves, torn
- 1 tbsp. freshly grated Parmesan

Directions

1. begin by beating the eggs into a small bowl first, then spinach and cheese should be added.
2. Use a cooking spray to spray a non-stick pan before pouring in the mixture.
3. Cook over medium heat for approximately 5 minutes, then turn with a spatula and continue cooking until the desired doneness is achieved.
4. Wait until it's cool to serve.
5. You can refrigerate any leftover amount for up to three days.

Cottage Cheese Breakfast

Ingredients

- 1/3 C. cottage cheese
- 1/3 C. plain yogurt
- 1/3 C. mashed blueberries

Directions

1. Get a bowl of appropriate sizes and mix all of the Ingredients in a bowl of medium size, and then serve.

Fishermen's Eggs

Ingredients

- 1 (3.75-oz.) can of sardine in water
- 2 Tbsp. fresh parsley
- 4 eggs

Directions

1. Preheat the oven to 375°F.
2. Get a casserole dish with a size that is enough to go in the oven or with a measurement of 8 inches by 8 inches and spray with a non-stick cooking spray.
3. Sardines should be drained; the water may be saved for another dish or used as a delightful garnish for your dog's meal.
4. Chop sardines and combine them with parsley in a bowl.
5. First, cover the bottom of the dish that has been created with the sardine mixture. (Either whisk the eggs and then pour them over the sardines or break each egg into a separate bowl of the mixture.)
6. Bake for 15 minutes or until the desired doneness of eggs is achieved.
7. Wait until the food is cool before giving it to your dog.
8. Store any leftovers in a refrigerator for three days or freeze them in an airtight container for up to six months, depending on your preference.

Raw Breakfast

Ingredients

- 1 egg
- 1 chicken liver, rinsed
- 1 oz. of muscle meat or heart
- ½ tsp. organic apple cider vinegar
- 2 Tbsp. plain yogurt, cottage cheese, or kefir
- 1 tsp. flaxseed oil
- ½ tsp. raw honey
- 1 frozen Raw Veggie cupcake, thawed

Directions

1. In a large dish, crack one egg and break up the shell into tiny pieces.

2. Add the chicken liver and the flesh from the bird's muscles, and then, just before serving, whisk in the honey, yogurt, flaxseed oil, and apple cider vinegar.

Deviled Eggs

Ingredients

- 6 eggs
- Water, as needed
- ¼ C. rinsed and cooked puréed chicken livers
- 1 tsp. organic apple cider vinegar

Directions

1. Put the eggs into a pot so that they can be covered with cover with water, and bring to a boil.
2. Continue cooking for one more minute with the lid on, then reduce the heat.
3. Cook for about 15 minutes, then turn off the heat and cover the eggs.
4. After removing the covers, run the eggs under cold water for a full minute.
5. While the water is running, crack the eggs and peel them.
6. Set eggs aside.
7. Cut eggs in half lengthwise, remove the yolks, and place them in a dish suitable for medium-sized portions. Along with the purée of chicken liver, add some apple cider vinegar to the bowl. The yolks, chicken livers, and vinegar should be mashed into a fine crumble.
8. Mix the egg yolk mixture together with the egg whites and mix well.
9. These delicious eggs may be stored in the refrigerator for up to three days (if they make it that long!).

Homemade Dog Side Dishes

Pepitas

Ingredients

- ½–2 C., depending on pumpkin size
- pumpkin
- 1 Tbsp. extra-virgin olive oil

Directions

1. Scoop seeds from the pumpkin
2. The seeds should be washed in a big colander, and any pulp should be thrown away.
3. Allow the seeds to dry out in the air on a baking sheet overnight after spreading them out.
4. Preheat the oven to 250°F. Put the seeds into a plastic bag with a zip-top and pour the extra virgin olive oil into the bag.
5. Shake the bag a little so that all of the seeds are covered with oil, then lay out the seeds on the baking sheet and put them into the oven
6. When golden brown, remove from oven.
7. Refrigerate after cooling.

Kanine Kale and Kiwi

Ingredients

- 2 tsp. coconut oil
- 1 minced clove
- 1 tsp. fresh ginger, peeled and minced
- 1 Tbsp. fresh oregano leaves
- 2 kiwis, peeled and chopped
- 1 bunch kale, washed and sliced into thin strips

Directions

1. Pour the coconut oil into a large pan and heat it over medium-high heat.
2. After adding the and ginger, continue to cook for another three minutes while stirring.
3. Stir in the oregano and kiwi and cook for an additional 2 minutes.
4. Add the kale and simmer for approximately 5 minutes or until the kale has wilted.
5. Take the food away from the heat and let it cool before giving it to your dog.
6. You can keep leftovers in the fridge for up to 5 days.

Arroz con Pollo

Ingredients

- ¼ C. olive oil
- 1 lb. boneless, skinless chicken thighs, diced
- 1 red bell pepper, seeded and chopped
- 2 tsp. dried oregano
- 2 tsp. dried rosemary
- ¼ tsp. powder
- 2 Tbsp. canola oil
- 1 (28-oz.) can crushed tomatoes
- C. water
- C. long-grain white rice
- ¼ C. chopped fresh parsley (optional)

Directions

1. In a large saucepan, bring the oil to a simmer over medium-high heat. After adding the chicken, continue to simmer for another eight minutes, stirring the pan regularly.
2. Cook the mixture for about 1 minute while stirring in the red bell pepper, oregano, rosemary, and powder.
3. Put in the rice, along with the canola oil, tomatoes, and water. Bring to a simmer over low heat. Then lower the temperature to low and continue to cook for another 20 minutes, or until the rice reaches a very soft consistency. Rice must be stirred on a regular basis to avoid becoming sticky.
4. Take the stew off the fire and let it cool down before adding any other supplements.

5. Add the parsley if you plan to use it, and serve immediately.

Chicken for Pulping's

Ingredients

- Tbsp. olive oil
- lb. boneless, skinless chicken thighs, cut into ½-inch cubes
- 1 Tbsp. dried rosemary
- ¼ tsp. powder
- C. Chicken Stock
- 1 C. grated carrots
- lb. potatoes, skin on, cleaned of eyes and green spots, diced into
- ½-inch cubes
- 1 C. frozen peas

Directions

1. The oil should be heated in a large stockpot set over medium-high heat. After approximately 8 minutes, add the chicken and continue to stir it periodically as it cooks so that all of the pieces get gently browned.
2. After adding the rosemary and powder, stir for approximately a minute until the mixture begins to smell pleasant.
3. Mix in the carrots, potatoes, and peas after adding the stock. Reduce the heat down to medium-low and continue to boil the potatoes for about 20 minutes or until they are fork-tender.
4. Re the pot off the heat and wait until the stew has cooled down before adding any further Ingredients.

Cluck and Quinoa Casserole

Ingredients

- Non-stick cooking spray
- C. Chicken Stock
- 1½ C. quinoa
- lb. ground chicken
- large eggs, beaten
- 1 C. grated carrots
- 1 C. grated zucchini
- 1 Tbsp. olive oil

Directions

1. Preheat the oven you want to use to 350 °F and coat a baking dish measuring 9 by 13 inches with non-stick cooking spray.
2. In a large bowl, fully mix the other Ingredients by stirring them until they are completely combined.
3. Place the mixture with a few spoonfuls in the baking dish that has been prepared.
4. Bake for one hour or until all of the liquid is absorbed and the mixture has reached the desired consistency.

5. Remove the food off the dish out of the oven and let it cool down before adding any more Ingredients or supplements.

Poultry Palooza

Ingredients

- Tbsp. canola oil
- 3½ lb. boneless, skinless chicken thighs, diced into bite-size bits
- 1 lb. chicken gizzards, chopped
- 1 lb. of chicken hearts, chopped
- ½ C. chopped chicken livers, about 3 oz.
- 1 Tbsp. finely chopped fresh rosemary
- ¼ tsp. powder
- 1 C. water
- 2½ tsp. Eggshell Powder

Directions

1. Prepare the oil in a big stockpot by heating it over medium-low heat.
2. After adding the chicken thighs, gizzards, hearts, and livers, as well as the rosemary, powder, and water, continue to boil the mixture for 20 to 25 minutes, or until all of the meat turns brown and is fully cooked.
3. After removing the pot from the heat, wait until the stew has cooled down before adding the eggshell powder.

Chicken Thighs and Tabbouleh

Ingredients

- C. Chicken Stock
- C. bulgur wheat
- ¼ C. canola or olive oil
- 2 lb. of boneless, with skinless chicken thighs, cut into 1-inch dice
- 1 medium red bell pepper that is seeded and cut into 1-inch dice
- 2 Roma tomatoes, cut into 1-inch dice
- ½ C. chopped fresh parsley or mint

Directions

1. Put the stock into a large stockpot and bring it up to a boil.
2. After weighing the bulgur wheat, place it in a big bowl and pour the boiling liquid into it.
3. Cover and let the mixture settle for one hour. The bulgur will become fluffy and light when it has absorbed all of the stock.
4. While the stock is simmering, bring the oil to temperature in the same stock pot you used for the stock over a heat setting between medium and high.

5. After adding the chicken and bell pepper to the stockpot, stir the contents of the pot on a regular basis for about eight minutes, or until the chicken is fully cooked and the bell pepper has become more tender.
6. Take the saucepan off the heat and then add the tomatoes and the parsley to it. Keep the tomatoes covered and let them steam, and become more pliable while you finish preparing the bulgur.
7. After adding the chicken mixture to the bulgur, give everything a quick stir to ensure that everything is well combined. Wait until the mixture has cooled down before adding any supplements.

Slow-Cooked Chicken and Barley

Ingredients

- 2 ½ C. pearl barley
- 2 lb. boneless, skinless chicken thighs, diced
- 2 C. finely chopped green beans
- 2 large carrots, diced or shredded
- 2 Roma tomatoes, chopped
- C. water
- 2 Tbsp. canola oil
- ¼ tsp. powder

Direction

1. Put all of the Ingredients into the saucepan of a slow cooker with a capacity of 6 qt., give it a good stir to incorporate everything, and make sure everything is distributed evenly.
2. Cook for eight hours with the temperature set to a low setting.
3. The stew should be allowed to cool down before any more Ingredients are added, after which the cooker should be turned off.

Stir-Fry and Rice

Ingredients

- ¼ C. canola oil
- 1¼ lb. of boneless, skinless chicken thighs, cut into ½-inch dice
- 2 medium carrots, grated
- C. cooked long-grain white rice (see Note)
- ½ C. thawed frozen spinach
- ½ tsp. grated fresh ginger
- ¼ tsp. powder
- large eggs, beaten

Directions

1. Heat the canola oil in a big heavy skillet for up to 5 minutes
2. Stir-fry the chicken and carrots for approximately 5 minutes until the meat is browned.

3. After adding the rice, spinach, ginger, and powder, continue cooking for another 5 minutes while tossing the mixture gently to avoid any of the Ingredients from being burned.
4. Stir in the eggs and cook for approximately 2 minutes, or until they have set.
5. Put on the heat and wait until the stir-fry has cooled down before adding any supplements to the food.

Turkey Minestrone

Ingredients

- 2 medium carrots
- 1 C. green beans
- ¼ C. canola oil
- 1½ lb. ground turkey
- large potatoes, skin on, cleaned of eyes and green spots, diced
- 1 C. frozen peas
- 1 (14.5-oz.) can cannellini beans, rinsed and drained
- 1 (14.5-oz.) can crushed tomatoes
- 2 C. dried egg noodles
- ¼ C. chopped fresh parsley
- ¼ tsp. powder
- C. water
- Freshly grated Parmesan cheese (optional)

Directions

1. Prepare the carrots by chopping them into large chunks and combining them with the green beans in a food processor. To get a finely chopped consistency, pulse the Ingredients between 8 and 12 times. (You can grate and chop the carrots by hand if you do not have access to a food processor.)
2. Put the carrots, green beans, oil, turkey, potatoes, peas, cannellini beans, tomatoes, noodles, parsley, powder, and water into the pot of a 6-quart slow cooker. Mix well. Cook for seven to eight hours with the temperature set to a low setting.
3. After turning off the heat source, wait until the stew has cooled down before adding any additional Ingredients.
4. If you want an extra-special surprise, sprinkle a little Parmesan on top of it if you want to.

Lazysagne

Ingredients

- C. water
- 1 lb. dried egg noodles
- 2 lb. of ground turkey
- 1 (14.5-oz.) can crushed tomatoes
- 1 (10-oz.) package frozen spinach, thawed
- 2 C. low-fat cottage cheese

- 1 tsp. dried basil
- 1 tsp. dried oregano
- ¼ tsp. powder

Directions

1. Put the water in a big stockpot, and bring it to a boil.
2. After putting the noodles and turkey in the pot, bring the water back to a boil while keeping the lid off to prevent it from spilling. Turn the heat down to low and continue to simmer the noodles while turning them regularly for a total of 12 minutes until they are tender.
3. After draining the noodles and turkey, save aside the broth for use in future recipes.
4. Put the noodles and the turkey back into the saucepan, then add the rest of the Ingredients and toss everything together to blend.
5. Before adding any more Ingredients, let the lasagne mixture cool to a temperature that is slightly higher than room temperature.

Turkey Meat Loaf

Ingredients

- Non-stick cooking spray
- 2 large eggs
- 1 (15-oz.) can crushed tomatoes
- ½ C. freshly grated Parmesan cheese
- ¼ C. finely chopped fresh parsley
- 2 tsp. dried basil
- 2 tsp. dried oregano
- ¼ tsp. powder
- 1 Tbsp. soy sauce
- 2½ C. quick-cooking rolled oats
- 2¼ lb. ground turkey

Directions

1. Turn the oven you want to use to 350 degrees Fahrenheit.
2. Apply non-stick cooking spray to the inside of either two loaf pans or one baking dish measuring 9 by 13 inches.
3. In a large bowl, whisk and mix the eggs, tomatoes, Parmesan, parsley, basil, oregano, powder, and soy sauce.
4. After completely combining the oats, turkey, and egg combination, transfer the resulting mixture into the baking pans that have been previously prepared.
5. Allow to bake for up to 45 to 55 minutes, or until a meat thermometer inserted into the middle of the loaf reads 170 degrees Fahrenheit.
6. After removing the beef loaf from the oven, wait until it has cooled completely before adding any supplements.

Beef and Bulgur

Ingredients

- 2 Tbsp. canola or olive oil
- 1½ lb. lean ground beef (85% lean)
- 2 medium zucchinis, finely chopped
- ½ C. finely chopped red bell pepper
- ¼ tsp. powder
- 3½ C. bulgur wheat
- 1 tsp. dried oregano
- C. water
- (14-oz.) can diced tomatoes

Directions

1. Grease a large Dutch oven and cook the ground beef, zucchini, bell pepper, and powder in the oil. Allow cooking until the meat is browned.
2. Cook for eight minutes, breaking up the meat with a spoon to ensure that it browns evenly and completely and tossing it periodically.
3. The bulgur and the oregano should both be added to the saucepan. Toss and boil the bulgur for approximately three minutes, being sure to toss it constantly until it becomes gently browned.
4. Mix in the water and the tomatoes while stirring. Bring to a simmer, then remove from the heat, cover, and let stand for twenty minutes or for all of the liquid to be absorbed, whichever comes first. First, give the stew some time to cool down before adding any supplements.

Hearty Beef

Ingredients

- 2 lb. ground beef (85% lean)
- 1 Tbsp. fresh rosemary, chopped
- ½ tsp. powder
- lb. beef heart (see Note)
- ¼ lb. beef liver, chopped (see Note)
- 2½ tsp. Eggshell Powder

Directions

1. In a large Dutch oven, mix the ground beef, rosemary, and powder, and cook over medium-high heat. Continue to cook the meat for another 5 minutes or until it starts to release its juices and fat.
2. After cutting the beef heart into cubes ranging from half an inch to an inch in size, put the Ingredients into a food processor and pulse them for ten seconds.
3. The beef heart should be added to the Dutch oven, stirring the mixture to blend.
4. After pouring in the beef liver, place the pan back on the stove and allow it to simmer for an extra 10 to 15 minutes, stirring three to four times, until all the meat is uniformly browned.
5. Bring the pot down from the heat, mix in the eggshell powder, and let the stew sit for a few minutes.
6. Let the mixture cool before adding any supplements.

Dog Treat Recipes

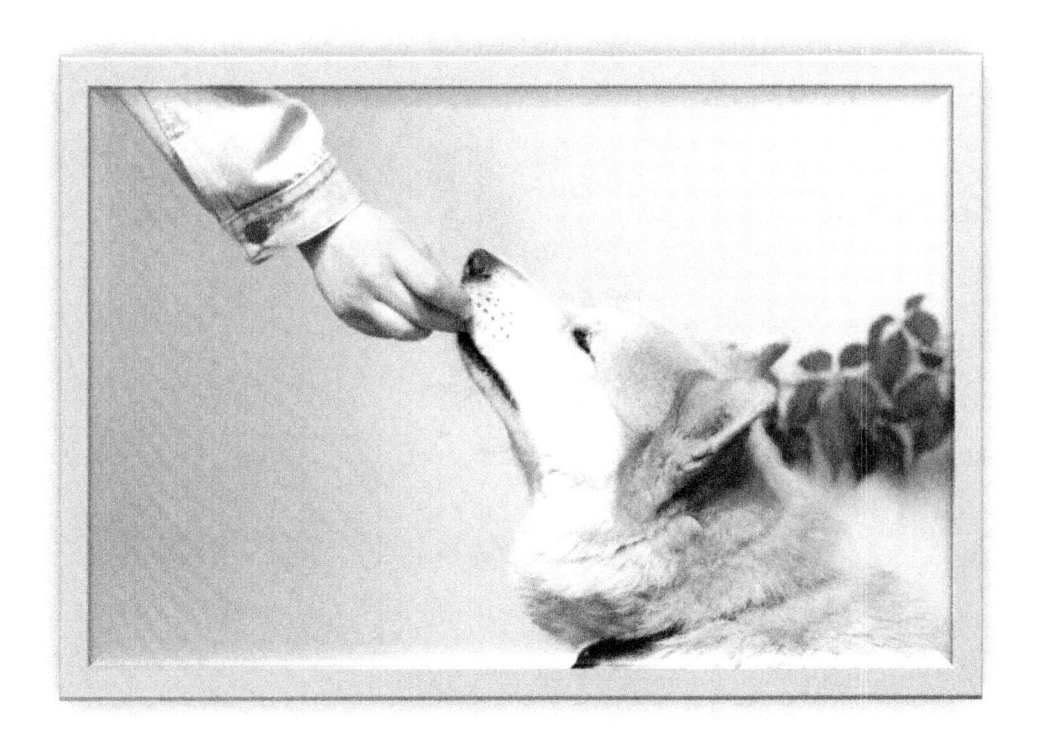

Peanut Butter Cookies

Ingredients

- 2 C. of flour (white or wheat)
- 1 C. of rolled oats
- 1/3 C. of smooth peanut butter
- 1 Tbsp. of honey
- ½ Tbsp. of fish oil (or flax oil)
- 1 ½ C. of water

Directions

1. To begin, preheat the oven to 350°F.
2. Mix the flour and oats together in a large bowl and stir until they're well combined. Pour in a C. of water and combine everything well again.
3. Mix all of the Ingredients together until they form a silky-smooth paste. Mix in the honey, peanut butter, and fish oil until all of the Ingredients are incorporated.
4. While stirring the mixture, gradually add the water until it has the consistency of dough. Continue stirring the mixture until it achieves the desired consistency.

5. Sprinkle a small amount of flour on the frying surface. Prepare a surface for rolling out the dough and roll it out to a 14-inch thickness.

6. A cookie-cutter is a great way to create a wide range of different shapes and sizes. After arranging the cookies in a single layer on a baking sheet, bake them for approximately 40 minutes.

7. Before serving, let the food cool completely.

Cheddar Dog Biscuits

Ingredients

- 1 C. rolled oats
- 1/3 C. margarine
- 1 C. boiling water
- 3/4 C. cornmeal
- 2 tsp. white sugar
- 2 tsp. beef bouillon granules
- ½ C. milk
- 1 C. shredded Cheddar cheese
- 1 egg, beaten
- 3 C. whole wheat flour

Directions

1. In order to get the best results, the oven should be preheated to 325 ° F. (165 degrees C). In a very large bowl, mix together the rolled oats, the margarine, and water that has been brought to a boil. Let stand for 10 minutes. Coat cookie sheets with butter.

2. Then, mix in the cornmeal, sugar, and bouillon as well as the milk, cheese, and egg well. Mix flour into the mixture. 1 cup at a time, and continue adding flour until a doughy consistency is reached.

3. Knead the dough on a lightly floured surface, adding extra flour as needed, until it is smooth and elastic.

4. The dough should be rolled out to a thickness of about a half-inch. Use a biscuit cutter to shape.

5. Bake for 35 to 45 minutes in an oven that has been prepared until the topping is golden brown. Wait until it's cool to serve. Put away in a container with a lid that is only partially on.

Dog snacks made with peanut butter and pumpkin

Ingredients

- 2 ½ C. whole wheat flour
- 2 eggs

- ½ C. canned pumpkin
- 2 Tbsp. peanut butter
- ½ tsp. salt
- ½ tsp. ground cinnamon

Directions

1. Preheat the oven temperature to 350 degrees Fahrenheit (175 degrees C).
2. In a bowl, combine the flour, eggs, pumpkin, peanut butter, salt, and cinnamon by whisking all of the Ingredients together.
3. The dough should be on the dry and stiff side, but you may add water as necessary to help make it more workable. Roll the dough into a roll with a thickness of one-half an inch. Pieces should be around half an inch in size.
4. Bake in the warmed-up oven until the substance is firm, approximately forty minutes.
5. Bake in an oven that has been warmed until the substance is firm, approximately forty minutes.

Pumpkin Ginger Dog Biscuit

Ingredients

- 3 C. whole wheat flour
- ½ tsp. ground ginger
- ½ C. pumpkin
- 1 big egg, beaten
- 1 Tbsp. coconut oil, melted
- ¼ to ½ C. of water

Directions

1. Set the oven temperature to 275 degrees F. Mix the flour and the ginger together. Mix pumpkin, an egg, and coconut oil. Add more flour and mix until it becomes a crumbly consistency.
2. Add water very gently, one tablespoon at a time, until the dough mixes well but is not sticky. On
3. On a surface dusted with flour, lay out the dough to a thickness of ¼ inch. Use a cookie cutter with a 3-inch to form the shape you want, then use a fork to make holes in the middle of the biscuit.
4. Place them 2 inches apart on an ungreased baking sheet. Bake for about 15 minutes or until the bottoms are gently browned. Place on a wire rack to cool. Put away in a container that prevents air leaks.

Chunk Chicken and Sweet Potato Treats

Ingredients

- 1 ¼ C. of ½-inch pieces of cooked chicken
- ½ C. of ½-inch pieces of cooked sweet potato
- 2 C. all-purpose whole wheat flour
- 1 C. evaporated low-fat milk
- ½ tsp. salt
- ½ tsp. baking powder
- 2 large eggs

Directions

1. Begin by preheating the oven to 350 degrees.
2. Mix all of the Ingredients thoroughly, making sure the chicken and sweet potatoes are evenly distributed. The potato should be thoroughly coated.
3. On to greased cookie sheets, spoon a teaspoonfuls of dough at a time.
4. Bake for 14 to 18 minutes or until browned.
5. Allow it to cool completely before placing it in an airtight container to keep it fresh.

Microwave Oatmeal Balls

Ingredients

- ¾ C. of non-fat dry milk
- ½ C. of all-purpose flour (white, whole wheat, barley, or potato)
- ¼ C. flaxseeds
- ¼ C. cornmeal
- 1 C. of quick oats
- 2 Tbsp. low-sodium beef bouillon powder
- 1/3 C. melted butter
- 1 large egg
- ½ C. warm water
- 1 C. quick oats, for coating treats

Directions

1. Combine the first six Ingredients thoroughly.

2. Mix in the butter, egg, and water until the dough comes together in a ball shape.
3. On a breadboard, spread out the remaining half cup of the quick oats.
4. Roll individual pieces of dough the size of marbles into balls and then coat each ball in oats.
5. Put 12 oat-covered balls on a heavy-duty paper plate (not a Styrofoam one), and set the plate aside.
6. Put the plate of treats in the microwave for 4 to 5 minutes at 50% power.
7. Take the food out of the microwave, let it cool completely, and store it in a container that won't let air in.

Peanut Butter, Honey, and Oat Cookies

Ingredients

- 1 C. crunchy (or extra-crunchy) natural peanut butter
- 3 C. quick oats
- 1/3 C. honey
- 1/3 C. low-sodium chicken or beef bouillon powder
- 1/3 C. warm water

Directions

1. Turn the oven temperature up to 350 degrees. To soften the peanut butter, put it in the microwave for a few seconds at a time.
2. Use a food processor or blender to turn 2 cups of quick oats into a coarse flour.
3. Mix all the Ingredients together well in a large bowl.
4. Sprinkle flour or more ground quickly on a breadboard before transferring the dough there. To form a ball with the dough, work it on the board until you can. Roll out the dough to about ¼ inch thick.
5. Cut the dough into desired shapes with a 3-inch dog bone cookie cutter.
6. Grease a cookie sheet and place the cookies there.
7. Bake the cookies for approximately ten minutes or until the bottoms have a golden-brown color.
8. Take out of the oven, wait until it has cooled completely, and then store it in a container that can keep air out.

Sunflower Sensations

Ingredients

- 2 C. all-purpose flour
- 1 C. ground roasted, unsalted sunflower seeds
- ¾ C. cornmeal

- 1 tsp. salt
- 2 large eggs
- ¼ C. evaporated low-fat milk
- ¼ C. vegetable oil
- ¼ C. molasses

Directions

1. Turn the oven temperature up to 350 degrees.
2. Put all of the Ingredients into a large bowl and mix them together. Use your hands to knead the dough until it is smooth and manageable.
3. Make a ball out of the dough, then place it on a breadboard that has been dusted with flour. It should be rolled out to a thickness of ¼ inch.
4. Cut the rolled dough into desired shapes with a 3-inch dog bone cookie cutter.
5. Put the cookies on cookie sheets that have been greased.
6. Bake for about 20 minutes or until the bottoms of the cookies turn a light brown color.
7. Store in an airtight container after it has been removed from the oven and allowed to cool completely.

Quick-and-Easy Cheese Circles

Ingredients

- ½ C. all-purpose flour
- 1 Tbsp. low-sodium beef bouillon powder
- 1 can refrigerated pizza crust
- ½ C. grated cheddar cheese

Directions

1. Preheat the oven to 350 degrees.
2. Place the flour and bouillon cube on a breadboard and combine them well with a mixing spoon. Take the pizza dough out of the container and spread it out with your hands in a gentle manner. Work the dough to straighten out any kinks or curves it may have, but be cautious not to tear it. Place it so that it is on top of the flour and bouillon mixture that is on the breadboard.
3. Make as many circles as you can using a cookie cutter that has a diameter of two and a half inches. After that, gather the leftover dough into a ball, re-roll it as if it were cookie dough, and cut out some additional circles using a cookie cutter.
4. Put each of the rounds on a cookie sheet that has been buttered. Sprinkle some shredded cheese on top of each cookie.
5. Bake the cookies for ten to twelve minutes or until the bottoms of the cookies have a golden-brown color.

6. Take out of the oven, wait for it to cool down thoroughly, and then store it in a container that doesn't allow air in.

Birthday Blueberry Pup cakes

Ingredients

- ½ C. high-quality dry dog food kibble
- 1 7-oz. package Jiffy Blueberry Muffin mix
- 1 C. fresh or frozen blueberries
- 2 large eggs
- 2/3 C. evaporated low-fat milk

Directions

1. Turn the oven temperature up to 350 degrees.
2. Ground the kibble into a coarse flour in a food processor or blender.
3. After grinding, measure out a half cup.
4. Mix the ground kibble from the dog food with the other Ingredients in a big dish until everything is properly mixed. The consistency of the batter should be similar to that of a little gritty cake batter.
5. Prepare the muffin tins by greasing them or lining them with the paper baking cup. (Avoid using baking cups made of foil; paper baking cups are digestible, so there's no risk even if your dog mistakenly eats one of them, but foil baking cups might create issues.) When filling the cup with the batter, fill each one half to two-thirds of the way.
6. Bake for 15 to 20 minutes, until the top is brown and golden. (The amount of time required to bake the treats may vary based on the Ingredients of the dry dog food that was used and the amount of food that was placed in each baking cup)
7. Take the cupcakes out of the oven, wait for them to cool down completely, and then store them in a container that can keep air out.
8. If you choose, you may top the cake with a layer of whipped cream cheese. You may either include a few blueberries into the icing or add a little bit of ground dog chow on top of each cupcake.

Valentine Hearts

Ingredients

- 3 C. all-purpose flour
- ½ C. non-fat dry milk
- ½ tsp. baking powder
- ½ tsp. salt
- 1/3 C. low-sodium chicken bouillon powder
- 2 large eggs
- 1 C. warm water
- 1 tsp. red food coloring or a red dye alternative (optional)
- 1 tsp. vanilla extract

Directions

1. Turn the oven temperature up to 350 degrees.
2. Place all of the dry Ingredients in a large bowl and stir them together until they are well combined. To make a firm dough, begin by adding the eggs, water, food coloring, and vanilla extract one at a time. Knead the dough for a total of two minutes using your hands.
3. Roll the dough into a ball and set it on a breadboard that has been dusted with flour. The dough should be rolled out to a thickness of approximately 1/4 inch.
4. To form the cookies from the rolled-out dough, cut out heart shapes using a cookie cutter measuring 2 inches.
5. Put the cookies on a cookie sheet that has been buttered.
6. Bake for up to 15 minutes or until the top is brown and golden.
7. Take the baked goods out of the oven, let them cool completely, and then store them in the refrigerator in an airtight container.

Potato Cranberry Christmas Cookies

Ingredients

- 2 C. potato flour
- 1 C. garbanzo flour
- 1 C. instant mashed potatoes
- 1 C. evaporated low-fat milk
- ½ C. applesauce

- 2 large eggs
- 1 C. whole frozen cranberries

Directions

1. Turn the temperature in the oven up to 350 degrees.
2. Combine all of the Ingredients, except the cranberries, and mix well. The dough will be dense and difficult to work with.
3. Drop by the half teaspoon onto cookie sheets that have been buttered. Put a full cranberry in the middle of each cookie and gently press it down so it doesn't move about. This will ensure that the fruit remains in place.
4. Bake for ten to fifteen minutes or until the bottoms are brown and golden.
5. Take out of the oven, wait until it has cooled completely, and then store it in a container that can keep air out.

Striped Peppermint Christmas Canes

Ingredients

- 3 C. all-purpose flour
- ½ C. non-fat dry milk
- ½ tsp. baking powder
- ½ tsp. salt
- 1/3 C. low-sodium chicken bouillon powder
- 2 large eggs
- 1 C. warm water
- 1 tsp. red food coloring or a red dye alternative (optional)
- ½ tsp. peppermint oil flavoring

Directions

1. Turn the temperature in the oven up to 350 degrees.
2. In a large bowl, combine all of the dry Ingredients and mix well. Add the eggs and water, and thoroughly combine everything.
3. The dough should be kneaded for a total of two minutes.
4. Roll the dough into two separate balls. Set one aside.
5. On a breadboard, press down on the top of the remaining dough ball to create a depression, then slightly flatten the ball. Place the food coloring and peppermint in the indentation, and then proceed to knead the dough once again, this time ensuring that the additional Ingredients are distributed evenly throughout the

dough. (You should use gloves if you are worried that any of the food colorings could transfer into your hands.)

6. After the dough has worked well, portion it out into a number of balls about the size of walnuts.
7. Also, roll balls of dough about the size of walnuts out of the ball of dough that was left aside. Maintain two distinct bowls for the two kinds of dough.
8. On the greased breadboard, roll out one piece of the peppermint dough until it resembles a long and thin sheet of dough. Proceed in the same manner with a piece of plain dough.
9. The two rolled-out pieces of dough should be twisted together, and then one end should be bent to make the twisted dough seem like a candy cane. Remove any uneven ends and put them on a cookie sheet that has been buttered. Continue doing so until all the remaining dough finishes.
10. Bake for 10 - 15 minutes or until the bottoms get a golden-brown color.
11. Take the baked goods out of the oven, let them cool completely, and then store them in an airtight container.

Peppermint Christmas Cookies

Ingredients

- 3 C. all-purpose flour
- ½ C. non-fat dry milk
- ½ tsp. baking powder
- ½ tsp. salt
- 1/3 C. low-sodium chicken bouillon powder
- 2 large eggs
- 1 C. warm water
- 1 tsp. red food coloring or a red dye alternative (optional)
- ½ tsp. peppermint oil flavoring

Directions

1. Turn the oven you plan to use to a temperature of 350 degrees.
2. In a large bowl, combine all of the dry Ingredients. After adding the eggs, water, food coloring, and peppermint, thoroughly combine the Ingredients. After that, knead the dough for a total of two minutes.
3. Roll the dough into a ball using your hands. Put the ball on a breadboard that has been dusted with flour. Roll out to a thickness of approximately one-quarter of an inch.
4. Use cookie cutters in the form of dog bones or Christmas tree shapes to cut the dough into various shapes.
5. Put the shapes on cookie sheets that have been buttered.
6. Bake for about 15 minutes or until the bottoms have developed a golden-brown color.

7. Take the baking pans out of the oven and, using a spatula, turn the cookies over so that they are facing the other direction.
8. Return them to the oven for another five minutes or until both sides have achieved a golden-brown color.
9. Take out of the oven, wait until it has cooled completely, and then store it in a container that can keep air out.

Chicken Liver Treats

Ingredients

- 1 lb. cooked chicken livers, chopped finely
- 1 C. cornmeal
- 1 C. all-purpose flour
- 2 large eggs
- ¼ C. vegetable oil
- ¼ C. warm water
- 1 C. cornmeal, for coating treats

Directions

1. Turn the oven temperature you plan to use up to 350 degrees.
2. Combine all of the Ingredients, ensuring sure that the liver is well covered in the mixture. The dough will have a firm texture.
3. First, divide the dough into portions the size of tsp., then roll each portion in cornmeal.
4. Put on cookie sheets that have been buttered.
5. Bake for 15 mins, or until the top is brown and golden. (Take care to prevent the bottoms from becoming burnt.)
6. Remove from the oven, wait until it has cooled completely, and then store it in the refrigerator in a container that is airtight.

Bisquick and Beef Treats

Ingredients

- 1 C. shredded or crumbled cooked beef
- 1 C. quick oats
- 1 ¼ C. of Bisquick baking mix
- ½ C. of evaporated low-fat milk

- 1 tsp. minced
- 2 to 3 tsp. of low-sodium beef bouillon powder

Directions

1. Increase the oven you plan to use to temperature up to 350 degrees.
2. All of the components should be well combined.
3. Place by rounded teaspoonfuls onto cookie sheets that have been buttered.
4. A little bit of beef bouillon should be sprinkled on each of the treats.
5. Bake for up to 15 minutes or until the top is brown and golden.
6. Remove from the oven, wait until it has cooled completely, and then store it in the refrigerator in a container that is airtight.

Basic Bones

Ingredients

- C. all-purpose flour
- ½ C. non-fat dry milk
- ½ tsp. baking powder
- ½ tsp. salt
- 1/3 C. low-sodium beef or chicken bouillon powder
- 2 large eggs
- C. warm water

Directions

1. Preheat the oven to 350 degrees.
2. Put All the dry Ingredients into a large bowl and mix. Slowly add the warm water and eggs and mix well. The dough will be stiff.
3. Using your hands, knead the dough until it is smooth and easy to handle, and then form it into a ball.
4. Place the ball on a floured breadboard. Roll the dough out to ¼ to 3/8 inch thick; slightly thicker is fine.
5. Use a 3-inch dog bone-shaped cookie cutter to cut out the dough.
6. Place the bones on greased cookie sheets.
7. Bake for up to15 to 20 minutes or until golden brown.
8. Remove the cookie sheets from the oven and, using a spatula, flip the bones over.
9. Return to the oven for approximately 5 minutes or until the bones are golden brown on both sides.
10. Take out of the oven, let cool thoroughly, and store in an airtight container.

Beefy Bacon Dog Bones

Ingredients

- 1 C. beef broth
- 1 C. crumbled cooked hamburger
- 4 Tbsp. bacon fat
- 4 to 6 slices bacon, well cooked and crumbled
- 1 large egg
- 4 C. all-purpose flour
- 1/3 C. non-fat dry milk
- ¾ tsp. baking powder
- ½ C. warm water
- 1 C. cornmeal for rolling out treats

Directions

1. Turn the oven temperature you plan to use up to 350 degrees.
2. Combine the first five Ingredients in a mixing bowl until they are well blended. Mix the flour, milk powder, and baking powder together in a mixing bowl.
3. Slowly add the warm water up to a half cup, and continue to stir the mixture until it forms a ball of dough. It's possible that the dough will be a little sticky.
4. Knead the dough until all of the Ingredients are evenly distributed throughout the dough.
5. Set the cornmeal on a breadboard, then place the dough on top of the cornmeal. Using your hands, press and flatten the dough. If it's sticky, give it a few turns in the cornmeal to get rid of the stickiness. Roll the dough using a rolling pin to a thickness of just more than one-quarter of an inch.
6. When cutting out the dough, use a bone-shaped cookie cutter that is at least three inches long.
7. Put on cookie sheets that have been buttered.
8. Bake for about 20 to 25 minutes, or until the bottoms have a golden-brown color. Take the dish out of the oven.

Crispy Cheese Circles

Ingredients

- 2 C. all-purpose flour
- ¼ C. grated fresh Parmesan cheese
- ¼ C. cornmeal

- 1 Tbsp. low-sodium beef bouillon powder
- 1 large egg
- ¾ to 1 C. warm water
- 1 C. cornmeal, for rolling out treats

Direction

1. Turn the oven temperature you plan to use up to 350 degrees.
2. First, combine the first four Ingredients, then proceed to add the egg and the 3/4 cup of heated water.
3. Combine in order to create dough. If the smoothness of the mixture is too dry, add some more water.
4. The cornmeal should be spread out on a breadboard. Make a ball out of one-half of the dough. Place it on top of the cornmeal, pat it down gently, and then flip it over so that both sides are coated with cornmeal. Roll the dough to form a thickness of 1/4 inch.
5. Use a 2 ½ inch diameter cookie cutter to cut out circles from the batter.
6. Put on cookie sheets that have been buttered.
7. Bake the bottoms for 15 to 20 minutes or until they have a golden-brown color.
8. You will need to repeat steps 3–6 with the remaining half of the dough.
9. Take the treats out of the oven, allow them to cool completely, and then store them in an airtight container.

Flaxseed Twists

Ingredients

- 2 C. all-purpose flour
- ¼ C. low-sodium beef or chicken bouillon powder
- ¼ C. flaxseed meal
- 1 large egg
- ¾ C. warm water
- 1 C. cornmeal, for rolling out treats
- ½ C. flaxseed meal, for rolling out treats

Directions

1. Turn the temperature in the oven up to 325 degrees.
2. Combine the first five Ingredients in a mixing bowl until they are well-mixed. After that, use your hands to knead the Ingredients until it comes together into a ball of dough.
3. Cornmeal and half a cup of flaxseed meal should be spread out on a breadboard. Place the dough ball on top of the mixture and gently press it down. Turn the dough over so that the cornmeal and flaxseed meal are distributed evenly on both sides. To get the dough to a thickness of about 14 inches, roll it out.

4. Cut the circle of dough into portions that are about 4 inches broad by using a knife that is very sharp.
5. Next, cut the dough in each piece into strips that are approximately an inch and a half broad. (The length and width of each strip will be 4 inches by ½ inch.) Turn each one of the strips a few times.
6. Put the strips on cookie sheets that have been buttered.
7. Bake for ten to fifteen minutes, or until the underside is a golden brown color.
8. Take out of the oven, wait until it has cooled completely, and then store it in an airtight container.

CONCLUSION

I hope you love giving your dog a homemade diet as much as I enjoy mine. The ease of knowing precisely what my family is eating surpasses the time and effort it takes to prepare it. In the same way that I would never provide food to my children if I didn't know exactly what was in it or where it came from, I do the same for me dogs. In my house, we treat our dogs like children and make sure they have the nutrition they need to live long and healthy lives.

Your dog may not appreciate the first dish you attempt, but don't be discouraged. Learning what he or she loves and dislikes will take some time. My recommendation is to experiment with a wide variety of foods. By following the advice and recipes in this book, it will be a great experience for both you and your dog.

Printed in Great Britain
by Amazon